EDUCATING BLACK MALES

SUNY Series,
Urban Voices, Urban Visions

Diane Dubose Brunner and Rashidah Jaami' Muhammad, Editors

EDUCATING BLACK MALES

Critical Lessons in Schooling, Community, and Power

Ronnie Hopkins

STATE UNIVERSITY OF NEW YORK PRESS

Production by Ruth Fisher
Marketing by Terry Abad Swierzowski

Published by
State University of New York Press, Albany

© 1997 State University of New York

For information, address the State University of New York Press,
State University Plaza, Albany, NY 12246

Library of Congress Cataloging-in-Publication Data

Hopkins, Ronnie, 1964–
    Educating Black males : critical lessons in schooling, community,
and power / Ronnie Hopkins.
        p.   cm. — (SUNY series, urban voices, urban visions)
    Includes bibliographical references (p.   ) and index.
    ISBN 0-7914-3157-6 (hc : alk. paper). — ISBN 0-7914-3158-4 (pb :
alk. paper)
    1. Afro-American young men—Education.   2. Afro-American men—
Education.   3. Educational innovations—United States.
4. Community and school—United States.   I. Title.   II. Series.
LC2731.H66   1997
370′.8996073—dc20   96-14999
                                                               CIP

10 9 8 7 6 5 4 3 2 1

In loving memory of Missionary Mollie Lee Windley Hopkins,
mother, teacher of humility, friend—my spiritual guide.
14 December 1930—28 September 1991

CONTENTS

Preface   ix

Acknowledgments   xv

1 Introduction: Black Males Are Dying—An Overview of the Crises Facing American African Males   1

2 "A Program of His Own": The Male Academy Movement   7

3 In the Midst of Storm: A Description of Models   29

4 The New Program: Approaches to Teaching Black Males   41

5 Black Male Culture, Power, and Resistance   63

6 Reclaiming Community, Renaming School: A Community Approach to Teaching Black Males   83

7 Who Will Teach Our Black Males?: "A Call to Action!"   95

8 Conclusion: Ain't Done with My Journey—Teaching for the Promise   109

Appendix A Black Male School and Program Features   115

Appendix B Addresses and Contact Numbers for Alternative Schools and Programs for American African Males   117

Appendix C Interview Excerpts from Phase One Study Participants   123

Appendix D Parent-Teacher Interviewing Instrument   131

Appendix E School Interviewing Instrument   133

Bibliography   137

Index   143

PREFACE

On 22 July 1991, I sat in the U.S. federal district courthouse in Detroit, at standing-room capacity, where mothers, fathers, teachers, community and church leaders, and others gathered to hear the federal court ruling on the constitutionality of the proposed Detroit Male Academy. The male academy was advanced as an experiment designed to provide a demonstration setting in which Detroit Public Schools might evaluate strategies for educating American African males. Ideally, the male academy was to focus primarily on the critical needs of American African males by immersing these students in a school environment that afforded them an opportunity to learn about their own ethnic heritage and to receive instruction reflecting and respecting cultural differences. The program was to serve as an intervention strategy promoting self-esteem and a motivation to learn. The paramount objective of the experiment was to prevent a new generation of young American African males from becoming yet another inner-city Black male statistic—high school drop-out, unemployed, absentee father, dope dealer, murderer, or victim of a violent crime.

Glaring eyes followed testimony after testimony as many of the parents of nearly six hundred young Black males who had already been accepted into the all-male schools awaited the ruling. Finally the decision was in. The deliberation was over. Everyone sat quietly on the edge of their seats. U.S. District Judge George Woods emphatically agreed that Detroit's young, inner-city males are severely at-risk, and he urged educators, community leaders, and lay persons alike to continue designing programs that would benefit these jeopardized youth. However, he reminded the school district that the school system fails to educate young women as well and that the very principle of the all-male academies runs counter to some of the most fundamental antidiscrimination laws in the country. He deemed the all-male academies unconstitutional and ordered the Detroit Public School Board to work out a compromise with the plaintiffs. After battles with national civic organizations and dissension among the Detroit District board members, the Detroit Public School Board voted not to appeal the decision.

As the judge adjourned the session, I observed the tearful eyes and harrowing expressions of Detroit mothers, fathers, and youth as they exited the courtroom as though departing a burial site after a funeral. And upon wiping the drops from my own eyes, I left the courtroom in anger. Absolutely outraged. How could anyone possibly say that such a worthwhile program was unconstitutional? When did loving and becoming one's brother's keeper become a crime? Had the plaintiffs not been made aware of the epidemic proportions in which American African males were dying in the classrooms and in the streets?

Since the federal district court decision, and after countless heated debates and discussions with feminist and womanist critics of the all-male academies, my anger has subsided very little. I still believe that the male academy has a place in the public school. Also, I fervently believe that given half a chance, such an academy could save American African males in great numbers, especially those who do not have the option of private education. Although the all-male academy concept in the public schools is, for the time being, a "dream deferred," it was not a battle waged in vain. Through international media coverage resulting from this national debate, parents, youth, community leaders, and educators throughout the world have become more knowledgeable of the plight of American Black males. Specifically, the male academy movement has yielded African-centered academies in Detroit, African American immersion academies in Milwaukee, pilot programs with all-male classes in Baltimore and Washington, D.C., and pull-out programs for tutoring, mentoring, and rites of passage for American African males within the public schools.

In fact, I consider this study a result of and reaction to my own experiences with the schooling of American African males. In 1987, I became an English teacher in the North Carolina public schools. Though I did teach in the traditional classroom for a short time, my most memorable and resonating teaching experience was at a program for "excluded students," where the student population was 98 percent male. These students were Black males dying—institutionalized in this academy for violation of school district codes (e.g., harboring weapons, selling drugs). And as national statistics continually broadcast, these Black males were at the very bottom of virtually every academic indicator and failing at disproportionate rates. The faculty who chose to teach in this nontraditional setting were diverse. I taught, quite literally, some of North Carolina's most inner-city, volatile, and criminal student populations. Even though the district deemed these students "excluded," I witnessed many of these Black males among our turbulent student population—even many known dope dealers and gang members—perform in the school chorus, introduce guest speakers at student assemblies, compete in district and national writing contests, and demonstrate their interest in learning, indeed major feats of accomplishment for these Black male castaways. Certainly not all of our students became perfect models of reform. We had our share who dropped out entirely, and we even attended several funerals. However, the vast majority of these Black male students developed a genuine interest in school. If I and other dedicated faculty and staff managed, with limited resources, to motivate and educate these Black males, why was the public school system failing at this task?

For three years I worked at the Detroit Malcolm X African-Centered Academy, initially proposed as a male academy. I was a mentor and site coordinator for Michigan State University's "My Brother's Keeper" Program, a university program designed to mentor inner-city youth in Detroit, a city with one of the highest dropout rates in the nation. Malcolm X Academy offered special attention and showed genuine compassion and concern for these inner-city youth, and the school proudly and rightfully boasts success in educating American African males (Watson and Smitherman, 1992). Malcolm X Academy and similar institutions recognized that in order to save Black males, specific strategies and pedagogies are needed. Clearly, while the status of the world's children in general is rapidly declining, and while increasing numbers of minorities in the United States are falling into seemingly irreversible tracks of poverty, the condition of American African males has reached horrifying proportions, and if they are to have a future, it is greatly dependent on their education.

This work seeks to address and understand the causes, processes, and difficulties in school politics which need to be taken
into account by school people and concerned lay persons alike if
they are to influence future healthy developments in the schooling
of American African males. It is a report and analysis of strategies
designed to educate American African males. It is a presentation of
interviews and observations of students, parents, teachers, secretaries, principals, and directors who are involved in alternative
schools and programs designed to educate Black males. Further,
this work is a presentation and analysis of "power." It is about the
power to defer dreams and ruin even the best-laid plans of unique
schooling opportunities for American African males. It is about
power relations in the classroom, in the schools, and in the community. As this study examines the empowerment of students, parents, teachers, secretaries, and administrators, it explores the processes by which these individuals develop more control over their
own lives and the skills and dispositions necessary to be critical
and effective participants, particularly in the schooling process, as
well as in society at large.

At a time when American African males rank lowest in virtually
every academic measure, and when the whole purpose and value of
our educational system is being questioned and new directions for
restructuring schools and educating our youth are desperately
sought, this work offers insight into how we can create more effective and empowering schools and classrooms. In order to do this,
this study first examines the larger social reality of American African males and analyzes theoretical contexts of educational practices in alternative education schools and programs for American
African males.

Chapter 1 overviews the devastating crises facing American African males and serves as a focal point to begin our conversation
about Black males, all-male academies, and the nature of "power."

In Chapter 2, I trace the highly controversial all-male academy
movement. Also, this chapter reviews the limited academic literature and media features which outline some of the arguments for
and against special schools for American African males.

Chapter 3 identifies schools and programs designed to educate
American African males, describes the models, and discusses the
pedagogy and techniques employed in these efforts.

In Chapter 4, strategies, methods, and male development processes currently employed by alternative education schools and programs are presented. This chapter highlights the most novel and innovative pedagogy used in teaching Black males.

Chapter 5 focuses on the "culture" of Black males. It discusses American African male resistance and sheds light on the historical treatment of Black males in traditional educational systems.

Chapter 6, primarily narrative, is an illustration of how alternative education schools and programs for Black males redefine schooling and community. It is a collage of lessons offered by administrators, parents, students, secretaries, and teachers regarding the teaching of Black males. This chapter provides a platform from which community voices, voices of "the people," discuss the issue of teaching Black males and what it means to be a part of the schooling of this population.

Chapter 7 is devoted to an analysis of the teachers of Black males in the public schools. This chapter demonstrates the dire need for reevaluation of teacher attitudes toward American African males. And it is "a call to action," a challenge to all educators to prepare themselves for teaching Black males.

Finally, in Chapter 8, I reflect on my research experience, thus articulating my personal journey to understanding how best to educate Black males.

No work has been completed which offers a comprehensive presentation of the voices and minds of the educational community who have designed, implemented, and currently maintain alternative education models for American African males. Furthermore, this study includes an exhaustive exposition of schools and programs designed to educate Black males, which should add to the academic community and to the existing body of literature a comprehensive, scholastic, and humanistic presentation of alternative education models designed to teach American African males. As well, I hope that this research will provide academic and emotional support for those of us who feel compassionately and have concerns about the effectiveness of strategies for teaching Black males. From this study, readers may gain a unique insight, thereby learning, understanding, and respecting that issues in teaching Black males come from "the people" whose daily lives are encompassed by these schools and programs.

Although the focus of this study is alternative schools and programs designed to educate American African males, the reader can assume that the teaching experiences, theories, and methods discussed are applicable to Black males in any learning environment. Further, many parents and teachers concern themselves only with the specific learning problems common within their teaching and learning environment and socioeconomic status; however, those who are responsible for teaching Black children in all environments should be aware of and sensitive to what is said in this text.

ACKNOWLEDGMENTS

I pour libations to the ubiquitous spirit of the Ancestors for paving the way for future generations, fighting injustices, surviving oppression, and "makin a way outta no way." I acknowledge the courageous American African men, women, and children and countless others who fight desperately to change and improve the educational system for Black males. I say to Black males in the struggle, "Keep marching upward and onward toward the light."

I salute and honor Dr. Clifford Watson and Mr. Ray Johnson of Detroit, Dr. Spencer Holland of Baltimore, and Mr. Bryce Baldwin of Raleigh, North Carolina, for dedicating their lives to ensuring the future healthy development of generations of American African males. Great thanks to Ms. Josephine Hill and Ms. Anita Sparks of Milwaukee for their guidance. Special thanks to the students, parents, administrators, and staff at Malcolm X and Paul Robeson African-Centered Academies, Detroit; the Center for Educating African American Males, Baltimore; Helping Hands Project, Wake County Public Schools, Raleigh, North Carolina; Martin Luther King, Jr. and Malcolm X African American Immersion Schools, Milwaukee; Morehouse Mentoring Program, Morehouse College, Atlanta; and "My Brother's Keeper" Program, Michigan State University, East Lansing.

I am highly appreciative of the inordinate patience and extensive kindnesses (which are beyond expression) due to my Michigan State University mentors, Professors Geneva Smitherman ("Dr. G"), Diane DuBose Brunner, William Johnsen, Marilyn Wilson, and Denise Troutman-Robinson. You have provided intellectual and emotional guidance which has allowed me to complete this project and envision many others. Especially to Dr. G for believing in me when I often doubted myself and for being a personal mentor, academic role model, and friend, I thank you. Many thanks to Drs. Angeletta K. M. Gourdine of Oregon State University and Rashidah Jaami Muhammad of Lansing, Michigan, for sharing your important suggestions.

To my students, colleagues, and friends in the Norfolk State University Spartan Family, thank you for your unwavering support. I acknowledge the NSU Department of English and Foreign Languages and the School of Arts and Letters. Special thanks to Drs. Gladys Heard and Thelma Thompson for untiring leadership. I acknowledge Drs. Bertha Escoffery, Maurice Henderson, and Rod Taylor, and Mrs. Barbara Collins McCall. For mentorship and friendship, I honor Drs. Wanda Mitchenor-Colston and Tina Marshall-Bradley. Especially do I thank my friend and colleague Dr. Deborah Goodwyn-Johnson for answering my desperate calls for assistance at any hour.

To my St. Louis family, Derrick Laney, Ruth Mathews, and Rosalynde, Harriett, and William Scott, I thank you for your love. I acknowledge my friends and colleagues at the University of Missouri—St Louis: Robin Clearmountain, John Works, Norman Seay, Jane Zeni, and Chuck Larson.

For preparing me "to serve" and to soar far beyond my tangible dreams, I acknowledge my alma mater, the North Carolina Central University. I recognize my mentors: Drs. Eugene Eaves, Ruth G. Kennedy, Patsy B. Perry, Phyliss Randall, Arthrell D. Sanders, John Sekora, and the late Dr. Charles H. Gilchrist.

To my soulmates and their loving families for standing by me through the thick and thin, I honor: Bill Whitaker of Frankfurt, Kentucky; Brenda McNeely of Lansing, Michigan; Gary L. Coleman of Detroit; Allen Sledge of Roanoke Rapids, North Carolina; David Malebranche of Schenectady, New York; John Gaither of Charlotte, North Carolina; Julius Dixon of Monrovia, Liberia; Harold Dixon of Charlotte, North Carolina; Roylisa Spell of Wilson, North Carolina; Susan Whitaker of Calverton, Maryland; Charles Braxton of Chicago; Clarence Stewart of Baltimore; Lawrence and Stephanie Poole of Philadelphia; and Quince and Janey Brinkley of Atlanta. I will treasure our friendships always.

I honor Leon Rouson, my fraternal, for your mentorship, friendship, and countless hours of encouragement. I salute my dearest colleague, Dr. Linda McNeely Strong-Leek; you are an unmovable structure in my life and I am grateful to have you as a friend. I thank you Vernon F. Sloan, my ace, my mentor, my kindred spirit. You are truly my foremost comrade.

To my adopted mother, Mrs. Ernestine "Aunt Tine" Garris of Monroe, North Carolina: Thank you for your love. My deepest gratitude and honor to my father, Charlie A. Hopkins Sr. of Bath, North Carolina, and to my siblings and their families, Shirley Moore and Sherry Hopkins of Chesapeake, Virginia; Evelyn Thomas of Houston; Willie Hopkins of Atlanta; Charlie Hopkins, Vernon Hopkins, John Hopkins, Jackie Lawrence, and Randolph Hopkins of Bath, North Carolina; Mollie Hopkins of Washington, North Carolina; and Terry Hopkins of Washington, North Carolina. I am forever grateful for your prayers, listening ears, financial support, and most importantly your steadfast belief in my completion of this endeavor. You have been my greatest teachers, my greatest source of energy.

Last, but not least, I give honor to the Almighty God, the grantor of life, health, and strength—the Lord and Savior of my life. To God be the Glory.

Ronnie Hopkins

1

Introduction: Black Males Are Dying— An Overview of the Crises Facing American African Males

Black males are portrayed . . . in a limited number of roles, most of them deviant, dangerous, and dysfunctional. . . . This constant barrage of predominantly disturbing images inevitably contributes to the public's negative stereotypes of black men, particularly of those who are perceived as young, hostile, and impulsive. Clearly, the message says: If they entertain you, enjoy them (at a safe distance); if they serve you, patronize them (and don't forget to leave a tip); if they threaten you, avoid them (don't ride the subway). Thus, young black males are stereotyped by the five "d's": dumb, deprived, dangerous, deviant, and disturbed. There is no room in this picture for comprehension, caring, or compassion of the plight of these young black men.

—Jewelle Taylor Gibbs, 1988, p.3

Education is considered to be the most accessible means for achieving social, political, economic, and cultural liberation in the United States. This traditionalist view accepts that public schools are vehicles of democracy and social and individual mobility. Educators and lay persons alike believe that the nature of public schools is the major mechanism for development of a democratic and egalitarian society. Historically, however, public schools in the United States have not contributed to the achievement of liberation for American Africans or for other minority populations. Rather than serve as vehicles for liberation for American African males and other people of color, public schools serve, at best, as agencies of social, economic, political, and cultural reproduction. As Henry Giroux (1988) asserts:

> Public schooling offers limited individual mobility to members of the working class and other oppressed groups, but it is a powerful instrument for the reproduction of capitalist relations of production and the dominant legitimating ideologies of the ruling group. (p. xx)

The reproduction of the proletariat and other oppressed groups by way of public schooling is clearly illustrated through an analysis of national poverty rates. From the following statistics, the American African adage "The more things change, the more they remain the same" accurately describes the reality of public schooling for many American Africans and well demonstrates the reproductive nature of public schools.

> Inadequate preparation in unequal schools and continued racial prejudice have trapped more than a third of African Americans in a cycle of poverty and a quality of life comparable to the Third World countries. (*State of Black America*, 1992, p. 142)

Data reported by the National Coalition of Advocates for Students (1986) show that American African children generally fall below grade level as early as elementary school, and the gap rapidly increases as they get older. American African children are tracked into slow learner groups at disproportionate rates, and they are three times as likely as their American European counterparts to be placed into classes for the educable mentally retarded, the behaviorally disturbed, and the emotionally impaired. Conversely, Black youth are half as likely to be placed in classes for gifted and talented students. Furthermore, they are often encouraged by school staff to employ courses of study that are less academically rigorous and less challenging and which tend to leave them trapped in general or vocational tracks much more often than American European students.

Shockingly, only 20 percent of American African eleventh graders could perform complex reading tasks as measured by the National Assessment of Educational Progress, while 53 percent of American European eleventh graders performed the task (Irvine, 1990). Although much improvement has been shown in reading and math in the past ten years, American African youth still score well below the national norm. In 1987, for instance, American African youth averaged ninety-nine points lower on the math section and seventy-nine points lower on the verbal section of the Scholastic Aptitude Test than their American European counterparts (Irvine, 1990).

Compared to American Europeans, American African students are twice as likely to drop out of high school and are suspended three times as often (Irvine, 1990). Although high-school graduation rates have improved and the American African population eligible for college has grown over the past twenty years, their rates of college entrance and completion have fallen since 1975 (College Entrance Examination Board, 1985). In fact, though overall dropout rates among American Africans have indeed declined, an alarming 15 percent of American Africans in the age group 16–24 had not graduated but were out of school in 1988, thereby expanding a virtually unemployable population (*State of Black America*, 1992). Statistics from the U.S. Census Bureau indicate that 21 percent of all 18–19-year-old and 25 percent of all 20–21-year-old American African youth had not completed nor were presently enrolled in high school (U.S. Census Bureau, 1981).

By virtually every measurable academic indicator, American African youth face a most heinous future in the traditional public schools. Yet, throughout the nation, American African youth and other minorities have no choice but to enroll in these systems which were designed to fail them. Because of educational failure, Black American youth face high rates of drug use, homicide, teenage pregnancy, crime, poverty, and unemployment. For instance, the National Urban League reported in 1992 that poverty rates for American Africans are the highest among any group in the United States. Lamentable statistics from 1988 suggest that 9.43 million

American Africans (31.6 percent) live below the poverty line. This percentage represents a ratio that has not changed since 1969, and one that is nearly two-and-a-half times the national average and more than three-and-a-half times that of American Europeans (*The State of Black America*, 1992).

Rather than serve as a vehicle to promote liberation, public schools have become structured support systems assuring social, political, cultural, and economic inequality for American Africans. Report after report painfully describes the inefficiency of traditional public schools in the United States.

In city after city, in virtually every "hood," you could well continue illustrating the tragic, endemic, and epidemic annihilation of American African males. In fact, volumes could be written about such atrocities. However, I am most interested in knowing where to go from here. The larger question is this: What is to be done about societal, political, economic, and cultural forces paralyzing the intellectual, economic, and cultural growth of the American African male?

School and community people believe change in traditional education for Black males is the most likely means by which to prepare them for world citizenship and liberation. Prior to engaging in the arguments for and against the all-male academies, it may be helpful to entertain recent critiques for mass schooling and views of public education. McNeil (1986) postulates that public schools have evolved historically as organizations serving basically two potentially conflicting purposes: (1) to educate citizens and (2) to process them into roles for economic production. To achieve the first goal, schools supply students with information and learning skills. However, because the intellects and skills levels of youth develop in ways that cannot be predetermined, the results are unpredictable. Secondly, schools process youth through stratified steps leading to predictable, marketable credentials for the workplace. The steps, and some of the outcomes, can be managed and controlled. Therefore, the school was organized to be in conflict with itself from the outset. This familiar line of argument is presented in both the deschooling tradition of Ivan Illich, which views organized schools as innately oppressive, and in some Marxist critiques of the public school as an agent of capital. McNeil sees public schools as conflicting institutions. Lawrence Cremin well illustrates this as he reminds us:

Schooling—like education in general—never liberates without at the same time limiting. It never empowers without at the same time constraining. It never frees without at the same time socializing. The question is not whether one or the other is occurring in isolation, but what the balance is, and to what end, and in light of what alternatives. (p. 132)

This analysis of the contradictory nature of American education leads to three critical questions regarding the education of Black males: (1) How do alternative education schools and programs designed for American African males "liberate"? (2) How do they "limit"? And (3) if the paramount goal for these schools and programs is to empower and to free the American African male, how, at the same time, might they render him a victim of "constraint" and "socialization"? Although this work analyzes alternative schools and programs designed for American African males in urban environments from the vantage point of schooling and power, it should be understood that the critical issues confronting American Africans in the inner city are many of the same problems facing Black males in rural and suburban communities as well. Thus, this view of education provides a useful dialectical context for understanding schooling for *all* American African males.

2

"A Program Of His Own":
The Male Academy Movement

The educational system as it has developed both in Europe and America [is] an antiquated process which does not hit the mark even in the case of the needs of the white man himself. If the white man wants to hold on to it, let him do so; but the Negro, so far as he is able, should develop and carry out *a program of his own*. [My emphasis]

—Carter G. Woodson, 1933, p.68

The male academy is "a program of his own." This chapter presents the theoretical plan for the male academy and the counterarguments posed by the opposition. A close examination of these critiques reveals that not only are the well-intentioned motives of the critics misdirected, but also that the three basic strategies directly respond to and nullify their claims. The three basic strategies which have been employed in an attempt to best educate American African males are as follows: (1) early intervention with the provision of American African role models, (2) the separation of students by gender, and (3) the infusion of African and American African history and culture within a multicultural curriculum. Those who oppose all-male schools and programs do so because they reject one or more of these three common components.

Despite the opposition to all-male schools and programs, urban school districts throughout the country have managed to design and implement various models of such schools and programs. For example, all-male schools and programs exist in Atlanta, Baltimore, Boston, Brooklyn, Cincinnati, Cleveland, East Cleveland, East Lansing, Detroit, Miami, Milwaukee, Minneapolis, New Orleans, New York, Oakland, Portland, Raleigh, Sacramento, San Diego, San Francisco, St. Louis, Tallahassee, Tampa, and Washington, D.C. (see Chapter 3 for description). Although Black male schools and programs exist in several cities, their operation is certainly not without opposition. The Black Male Academy Movement has aroused considerable debate and raised issues of racial segregation, gender separation, and the validity and appropriateness of Africentricity in the curriculum.

A typical critique of all-male schools as segregationist is revealed by Alfred Yates, of University of Oxford Department of Education, who asserts:

> Grouping on the basis of race . . . encourages racial discrimination whereas an integrated school providing shared experiences and a common purpose at least affords an opportunity for the development of tolerance and understanding. (Soderman and Phillips, 1986, p. 18)

Some civil rights groups and activists agree. They express vehement opposition to the very possibility of all-male schools and programs. The National Association for the Advancement of Colored People (NAACP) insists upon retaining its historical opposition to "school segregation." Detroit activist Horace Sheffield Jr. (1991) asserts that after decades of fighting for civil rights gains, he can find no rationale for bringing any form of segregation back into the schools. Likewise, Duke University historian John Hope Franklin fears that the "drawn lines of the resegregation of schools would yield an unhealthy society" (Soderman and Phillips, 1986, p. 13). These activists argue that desegregation in any form could lead to forced resegregation of the schools, whether through schools of choice or other means.

Dr. Kenneth Clark, a psychologist whose research guided the

1954 Supreme Court decision banning school segregation, has also expressed his concerns about proposals for all-male schools: "For adults to impose this nonsense on children, [that is,] reemergence of schools that are intentionally racially segregated and about separating students on the basis of sex, is academic abuse" (qtd. in The Abell Report, 1991, p. 3). Another critic, William Chester Jordan, professor of European history at Princeton, declares that

> separation not only impoverishes, it must lead to a distressing emphasis on 'otherness.' Do we have to hurt the black boys in this misguided effort? We have crippled enough children in anger. Must we do so with misguided love? (qtd. in The Abell Report, 1991, p. 3)

In contrast, Daniel Frey (1992), in his senior thesis research at Princeton, summarizes the argument against racial segregation in relationship to all-male schools and programs, and suggests that

> resegregating, even if for the altruistic goal of aiding black males, would set society back several decades in the struggle for racial equality. This is not because school desegregation has worked so well for African American students, but because resegregating schools could pave the way for future abuses. (p. 87)

Frey posits that the resegregationist argument is based purely on conjecture. Just as proponents are criticized for their argument that separate schools for boys could be a solution to the miseducation of Black males, opponents present the hypothesis that these schools necessarily would lead to abuses for young males. Further, Frey (1992) contends that this criticism of all-male academies is misguided and unwarranted, as all-male academies are open to children of any race. Racial segregation can hardly be considered a substantial issue since, as Frey establishes, the overwhelming majority of school districts with such programs are majority American African. And increasingly, America's major urban centers are majority Black, or people of color. American Africans are majorities in fifteen major cities, including Atlanta, Baltimore, Detroit, New Orleans, and Newark. In 1980, East St. Louis had a population which was 96 percent American African. Several cities, including Baltimore, Detroit, New Orleans, and Washington, D.C., have American African enrollments in their public schools higher than 75 percent. Nationally, 63 percent of American African students attend schools that are less than 50 percent American European. More than 80 percent of American African students attend schools which are predominantly American African (Frey, 1992, p. 88).

It is clear that racial segregation is not a substantial argument against implementation of alternative education programs for American African males. It is highly unnecessary for these programs, which are predominantly Black, to seek further resegregation.

Early Intervention

Early intervention strategies and the provision of male role models have been by far the least challenged features of the all-male academy. Dr. Keith Griger, president of the National Education Association, comments on the need for early intervention in the schooling process:

> School reform in the 1980s has put the emphasis at the wrong end of the educational spectrum. We don't lose students in college. We don't lose them in high school. We don't even lose them in middle schools. Any elementary teacher can identify those students who need additional assistance in the early years to ensure their success later on. We must start reforming our education system at the ground floor. If we're serious about improving the knowledge, skills, and numbers of our high school and college graduates—we must make dramatic improvements in class size and other learning conditions for young children. Most of all, we must re-examine our attitudes about those who teach children in the critical years. They are the professionals who build the foundation on which our house of education stands. (qtd. in Holland, 1991, p. 41)

Similarly, Morgan State University professor and director of the Center for Educating African American Males, Spencer Holland, observes that although American African male students at all grade levels are "at-risk," it is during the primary years that a child's whole attitude toward the educational enterprise is established. Holland, a psychologist, asserts that:

These little boys know how to do school work, but we've got to show them that it is appropriate because he comes into that school building with a set of male behaviors that he's picked up in the street. These behaviors are generally inimical to the school setting. (Interview, 1993)

He further points out that being retained in first and second grade is one of the most traumatic and emotionally destructive experiences a child can endure. It is no longer mere speculation that many, if not most, American African male students who drop out of the educative process often do so emotionally and psychologically by the end of third grade. For a child to be labeled incapable of learning during this most critical time of his life is indefensible and could well end the motivation for that child to achieve (Interview, Holland, 1993).

Dr. Clifford Watson, principal and founder of the Detroit Malcolm X Academy, agrees that early intervention is a major key in assuring success for American African males. From his experiences in educating urban Black males, Watson is confident that by intervening with young, Black males at an early age and by providing them with positive American African male role models who counter the stereotypical male models of the street, Black males can be better assured quality education:

We must start with children at an early age. The problem is, and research validates this, that we begin to lose male students around third grade. . . . So if you get these boys into reading in kindergarten, and you keep that going, then when they get in the eighth grade, do you think that they are going to be reading on the fourth grade level as many of them do now? (qtd. in Gourdine and Smitherman, 1992, p. 6)

Holland concurs that young American African males are yearning for positive, Black male role models to counter the "dope boy in the hood" image. He believes that first through third grades are the critical periods when male role models should be involved:

Bring men in to show little boys it's alright to sing songs, to play games, "the red sits down and the yellow stands up" and all of those techniques that primary grade teachers use to convince children that it is really, really something important for you to learn these squiggly lines we call letters and numbers. (Interview, 1993)

The belief is that young boys bring the attitudes of the streets into class with them. They see their peers devalue the entire academic enterprise, interact primarily with women teachers, and very soon begin to assign feminine characteristics to these endeavors and occupations. In the macho culture of the street, these are seen as negatives (Gibbs, 1988).

On Issues Of Gender

A recurring argument against all-male schools is that the schools discriminate against females. This argument has gained legal precedent due to litigation brought against the Detroit Public Schools regarding the Male Academy by the American Civil Liberties Union (ACLU) and the National Organization of Women's Education and Defense Fund (NOW). This 1991 federal district court case determined that the Detroit Male Academy discriminated against females based on Title IX of the 1972 Education Amendment, which states that gender discrimination in the public school is unconstitutional. Most schools and programs that were initially proposed as all male currently admit females because of legal challenges; however, some schools do conduct single gender classes on an experimental basis (see chapter 4 for complete descriptions). Proponents of all-male schools argue that single gender schools and classes will allow them to better construct a school mission and provide curriculum, management, and instruction that will directly deal with American African males in hopes of preventing them from entering the cycle of problems inherent to inner-city American African males.

According to Walteen Truely, a representative of NOW, the Detroit Public School Male Academy concept excluded women from an excellent program that proposed incorporation of a culturally relevant curriculum and provided significant counseling strategies geared to directing children to positive futures. Further, Truely claims that all-male schools are potential breeding grounds for negative attitudes about women which males may acquire from being educated in an all-male setting:

> The research on all-male schools show that young men who come out of those experiences building their self-esteem unfortunately do so on a sense of superiority to women. Young women need to see healthy role models who have positive attitudes. (*The Dayna Eubanks Show*, August, 1991)

Executive Director of the ACLU of Michigan, Howard Simon, agrees that educational opportunities and benefits in the Detroit Public Schools should be made available to males and females (*The Dayna Eubanks Show*, August, 1991). While both the ACLU and NOW recognize that all urban school children in this country are in crises, Simon and Truely maintain that their paramount concern is that females be allowed the same opportunities as males.

The sincerity and motive of such claims is questioned by proponents of the all-male academy. Dr. Watson, principal and founder of the Detroit Malcolm X African-Centered Academy, points out that for at least ten years several *all-male* and *all-female* programs have existed in the Detroit Public Schools (*The Dayna Eubanks Show*, August, 1991). Included among these schools are the Detroit Westside Development Center, a program designed for boys on the expulsion track, and three female high-school programs designed for pregnant women. These single-gender programs have been maintained in the Detroit Public School without challenges from NOW, ACLU, Detroit residents, or any other group or organization. Watson considers this inconsistency a camouflage for institutionalized racism and a perpetuation of American European hegemony:

> Certain institutions will continue to move throughout history to suppress young African American males. We see it here in terms of the district trying to do something positive for the love of children. It's not about girls against boys. It's not about Black against white. It's about salvaging our young people so that they can be productive citizens. (Interview, 1993)

Yet another response regarding allegations of gender discrimination is posed by former Detroit Public Schools Superintendent Deborah McGriff, who contends that the civil organizations who legally challenged the male academy illustrate expansive inconsistences. She argues that the notion that it is unconstitutional to segregate American African male students is a major contradiction in terms, because

> if you'll look at special education classes in this country where they label children as emotionally disturbed, most of these students are African American males and neither one of these organizations [ACLU and NOW] came forward to petition or protest that. Look at classes for the gifted and talented, African Americans are historically excluded from those classes in integrated settings, but no one came forward to argue against that. But when we say as a school system that we want to do something positive, we want to establish an experimental program to see if we can discover ways to educate all children, we are challenged. And no we don't know if this program will work. But what we in Detroit do know is what we're doing now doesn't work. (*The Dayna Eubanks Show*, August, 1991)

American African educator and filmmaker Jawanza Kunjufu (1991b) supports gender separation as an attempt to "do something positively for Black youth." He explicates the need for gender separation for American African males in light of the criticism that all-male schools exercise a bias towards females:

> We are very much aware that African American females are also underachieving, leading the world in teen pregnancy and are paid less than other American workers. Separate schools for teen mothers during and after pregnancy are currently in existence in Detroit. The reality is more males go to special education, remedial reading, are suspended, drop out, and go to prison than females, who exceed African American males in college. (p. 88)

Watson agrees that American African females are living in dire circumstances in the inner-city, just as the American African males; however, he acknowledges that there are strategic reasons for targeting American African males:

> The entire Black community, both males and females are suffering. . . . However, when we look at homicide in Detroit, girls are not killing girls. Black males are killing Black males *and girls.* (*The Dayna Eubanks Show*)

American African psychologist Maulana Karenga supports the all-male concept, provided the goal is to prepare American African males for world citizenship:

> Part of our education is learning to live, dream and work together. But I accept the need for a transitional arrangement in which Black boys are given particular attention in a context in which they are compelled to confront themselves both in intellectual and moral terms, and given added assistance both in terms of academic excellence and social responsibility. (qtd. in Wiley, 1993, p. 21)

Both opponents and supporters of the all-male academy have predicted the outcomes and effects of this single gender environment. Yet little research has been done on the topic of single-sex education in general, and virtually none on single-sex education in the national American African community. Prior to the research of Sadker and Sadker (1994), much of the existing literature neither fully confirmed nor denied the claims of opponents and proponents. For example, Daniel Frey (1992) observes that

> there are extreme variations in the conclusions and interpretations of single-sex/co-ed comparisons. For achievement and affective outcomes some studies favor coed schools, some favor single-sex, and others find no differences. (p. 61)

More conclusive findings from other researchers report that minority females benefit most in single gender settings:

> Recent research supports the academic effectiveness of single-sex classrooms and schools for male and female students, irrespective of race. . . . Moreover, minority females make more

cognitive gains from single-sex schooling than minority males. Finally, while all-male classrooms and schools seem to stress discipline more than do coeducational environments, discipline problems decrease considerably in single-sex schools. (qtd. in Frey, 1992, p. 61)

The study by Harvard researchers David Sadker and Myra Sadker (1994) reports on the effectiveness of education in single-gender settings. In their twenty-year study, *Failing At Fairness: How America's Schools Cheat Girls*, Sadker and Sadker, a wife-and-husband team, present their observations of classrooms and their analyses of teacher and student behavior. They conclude that teachers and students exercise gender bias and that this inequity disadvantages girls. The researchers assert that often sexism is illustrated "in a quick, jarring flash within the hectic pace of the school day" (p. 2). From an observation of one of the "elite" and "expensive" private schools in Washington, D.C., the researchers present what they deem a quintessential example of sexism in an academic setting:

> Two second graders are kneeling beside a large box. They whisper excitedly to each other as they pull out wooden blocks, colored balls, counting sticks. So absorbed are these two small children in examining and sorting the materials they are visibly startled by the teacher's impatient voice as she hovers over them. "Ann! Julia! Get your cottinpickin' hands out of the math box. Move over so the boys can get there and do their work." (p. 2)

The researchers remark that this incident is not difficult to interpret. And they insist that putting the situation in terms of race makes the teacher's actions more distinct. They explain:

> Picture Ann and Julia as African American children moved away so white children can gain access to the math materials. If Ann and Julia's parents had observed this exchange, they might justifiably wonder whether their tuition dollars were well spent. (p. 2)

In the Sadker and Sadker study, trained raters coded classrooms in math, reading, English, and social studies. They observed students from different racial and ethnic backgrounds and lessons taught by men and women teachers of different races. Among these "destructive" teaching methods, the Sadkers observed that even a "no-nonsense veteran" teacher like Mrs. Zajac of Mt. Holyoke, Massachusetts, illustrates sexist behaviors in the classroom. Mrs. Zajac, in her discussion of inventors and discoveries writes, on the board:

Elias Howe	sewing machine
Robert Fulton	steamboat
Thomas Edison	light bulb
James Otis	elevator
Alexander Graham Bell	telephone
Cyrus McCormick	reaper
Eli Whitney	cotton gin
Orville and Wilbur Wright	airplane

A girl raises her hand and asks, "It looks like all the inventors were men. Didn't women invent anything?" The teacher does not add any female inventors to the list nor does she discuss new scholarship recognizing the involvement of women in inventions such as the cotton gin. (p. 7)

The researchers postulate that this type of biased instruction is more subliminal than overt; at any rate, it is destructive to females. Clearly the Sadkers' position is that if teachers are appropriately trained to recognize when they are demonstrating preferential behaviors during instruction, and sensitized to these inequalities, their patterns of giving boys more attention will disappear.

Given that the American public school has traditionally been a constituent of systematic white male hegemony, I have no doubt that America's schools do cheat girls. However, Sadker and Sadker need to be explicit about which girls are being cheated and who is being favored. If indeed females are being cheated, certainly not all males are favored in this analysis of "America's schools." Although the Sadkers suggest that their research includes students and teachers of different races and ethnicities, it is overwhelmingly evident that their work is culture specific, by race and class. Their research appears consistently to contain elitist and separatist overtones, especially relating to the description of the research sites. Even in their own description of the research sites, the researchers highlight the fact that the studies were conducted at "prestigious," "private," and "Ivy League" places like Mt. Holyoke, Massachusetts; thus, they obviously exclude the countless number of girls who are not privy to these "institutions" (p.2). Additionally, when major cities with high populations of American Africans are mentioned, such as Washington, D.C., and Brooklyn, they are done so only in conjunction with private academies or with universities, again emphasizing that this study excludes children based on race and class.

The focus of their research is a feminist approach to analyzing *American* educational systems, and they claim that their research is multicultural and multiethnic. Yet, in their analysis they fail to mention ethnic biases which favor American European children in general, and the ethnic biases found in their own research. Directly, in the aforementioned list of inventors and discoverers, the Sadkers point out that all of the inventors listed were male; significantly, they failed to mention another characteristic common among the inventors and discoverers listed: They were all dead, White, and male. And contrary to their notion of sexism, which they deem subliminal, this type of racial and ethnic bias is not at all subliminal. Indeed, it is quite overt. Perhaps American European females leave this schooling exercise believing that no American European female inventors or discoverers existed, but American African females, American African males, and other minorities go away having no cultural, racial, or ethnic validation whatsoever. For example, there was no mention of American African inventors, such as, Garret Morgan, the inventor of the traffic light, or Madame C. J. Walker, the inventor of the straightening comb and entrepreneur of hair industries. This type of validation should not be limited to gender, but should include the cultures of the "Other," discussing the issues of language diversity, ethnic and racial diversity, ablebodiedness, heterosexism, homophobia, and other issues of culture.

To the issue of giving more attention to males than females, Sadker and Sadker assert:

While boys rise to the top of the class, they also land at the bottom. Labeled as problems in need of special control or assistance, boys are more likely to fail a course, miss promotion, or drop out of school. (p. 195)

They maintain that because of the "special" attention boys need, schools considerably favor them over girls and make special reparations to accommodate their unique needs by providing sports clubs, leadership training, and academic incentives (p. 195). Perhaps providing unique programs and opportunities for males may be true for American Europeans. However, according to the research for Black males, *American* public schools do not provide special attention and programming for Black males with the exception of tracking, which has been proven to be disadvantageous. Contrary to the Sadkers, any special treatment given to Black males in schooling often results in disproportionate suspension rates, lower academic achievement than their American European counterparts, frequent referral to learning and emotionally exceptional classes, and exclusion from gifted and talented programs, leading to eventual drop-out. In all *fairness*, this analysis of *America's* schools should read: *Failing at Fairness: How America's Schools Cheat American European Girls, Isolate American African Girls, and Terminate American African Males*. This illustration of a Eurocentrist approach to research and education has raised major concerns in the national American African community, and serves partly as the basis for an African Centered focus in education, namely, because it allows individuals to conduct "American" studies and totally ignore American African positions and other cultural perspectives.

Further, I am not completely without sympathy to the overall line of argument presented by those who oppose alternative education schools and programs for American African males because they deem them sexist. However, I reject the argument of Truely that schools and programs designed for American African males necessarily cheat girls because young men who come out of this educative experience may build their own self-esteem and self-confidence "on a sense of superiority to women" (The Dayna Eubanks Show, August, 1991). The critics, such as NOW and ACLU, have presented their objection to the all-male academy based on portraits of tendencies, not certainties, and their concerns raised are pure conjecture. Contrary to their speculations, there are educators, parents, and others who believe that all-male schooling for American African males may very well promote equality, reshape social structure, and narrow differences between social groups. Clearly, the paramount rationale for gender separation in alternative education schools and programs for American African males is related to crisis intervention; that is, it is a promotion of self-esteem building and motivation for learning for Black males in single-sex settings.

Africentricity in the Public School

In addition to the criticism that all-male schools discriminate on the basis of race and gender, critics further question the incorporation of Africentricity into the public school curriculum. Through an analysis of various critiques of Africentricity, I will demonstrate that the object of these criticisms does not in fact exist as monolithically as critics charge. The major criticism characterizes Africentrist scholarship as irrational and suggests Africentrist scholars should not provide academic foundations for curricula for primary and secondary education. Further, some scholars claim that the Africentrist view presents the civilization of Europe as corrupt, aggressive, and inhumane—inferior in every way to African civilization, which is visualized as a paradise of communitarianism, cooperation, and spirituality.

The Manhattan Institute reveals in a 1994 study of Africentrist philosophy that:

> (1) There is no empirical evidence that teaching about African civilization improves the academic performance, personal situations or life chances of Black students. (2) The content of the major Afrocentric curricula is often racist and frequently in error. (3) There are better and more honest ways to teach about African history. (Tobin, 1994, p. 18)

Harvard University W. E. B. Dubois Professor of Humanities and chair of the Afro-American Studies Department, Henry Louis Gates Jr., contends that Africentrist theory is dangerous and is inundated with overgeneralizations wherein Africentrist scholars make claims to what is African and what is not African before adequate research is done (Tobin, 1994). In a recent issue of *The Journal of Blacks in Higher Education*, Gates and other scholars offer their views on Africentricity in the public school:

> I worry that the sort of cognitive relativism promoted by many Afrocentrists eventuates precisely in . . . epistemic segregation, where disagreement betokens only culpable failure to comprehend. This explains my own skepticism about such approaches. (Gates, 1994, p. 42)

Princeton University Religion Professor Cornel West remarks that he is distinctly to the right of the Africentrist school. He views the Africentrist Black nationalist position "gallant but misguided" (qtd. in *Journal of Blacks in Higher Education* p. 9). Other scholars consider incorporation of Africentrist theory in the public school curriculum an academic and social restraint for Black children. For example, Diane Ravitch, a 1994 visiting fellow at The Brookings Institution in Washington, D.C., asserts:

> If a student or professor in higher education wants to immerse himself or herself entirely in the history/culture/language of a particular nation or region or continent, that is his or her choice. I think it is a different matter altogether when children in public school are taught in an Afrocentric school, where they may not be studying the kind of math and science that are studied in the schools of all developed nations; if that is the case, as it apparently is in some schools, then their teachers do them a disservice by failing to prepare them for life in a technological, multicultural society. (p. 42)

Other scholars share this view of the Africentrist curriculum in the public schools. Edward N. Luttwak (1994) states:

> We are very far from the harmless inclusion of African folk tales in first grade readings, or the useful addition of Chinua Achebe's novels in high school English Lit. Real confusion is being inflicted on children often already handicapped by poverty, disorder, and ignorance at home. (p. 43)

For many academics and educators, then, Africentrist theory is a fluke that yields absolutely no value in the public school curriculum. Such critics argue that Africentrist views do not even attempt to enhance American education. Instead, as the Manhattan Institute study claims, "these propagandists, like the Nation of Islam and the Ku Klux Klan, believe that race is the most important attribute of a person, and they believe that Blacks are inherently morally superior to whites" (Charen, 1994, p. 11). It is indeed appropriate and necessary for scholars to deconstruct one another in the academy to ensure that sound scholarship is made available worldwide. Further, it is academically healthy to question all works and challenge any claims presented as "truth." Africentrists are not immune to such challenges and certainly should be held accountable for their scholastic claims. At the same time, however, critics of Africentrist philosophies are in dire need of deconstruction as well.

An important observation is that critics of the Africentrist philosophies present monolithic arguments, such as the aforementioned claims by the Manhattan Institute which reduce all "Africentrist" theories and methods into a single conglomerate. This criticism presupposes that there exists a single Africentrist theory or philosophy. In fact, there are variations of Africentrist theory. For example, Gates, a major critic of Africentrist theories, states:

There is not just one group of Afrocentric people in Black studies. I would say that some of the things I advocate are Afrocentric, but I am certainly not in the same camp as Molefi Asante and all these guys. (qtd. in Tobin, 1994, p. 5)

Gates believes that "Asante and these guys" have claimed sole rights to the title of "Africentricity." The Gates Africentrist camp holds as its principal philosophy the need to integrate more African and American African studies within "standard" American curricula. These scholars view other Africentrist approaches as separatist, divisive, and counterproductive. Gates notes that these approaches "ghettoize" academia and "allow students and faculty to sit around and argue whether or not a white person can think a Black thought" (qtd. in Tobin, 1991, p. 5).

Professor Molefi Asante, chair of the African-American Studies Department at Temple University, is a leading theorist of Africentrism. Asante argues that the research of scholars like Gates presents "white studies conducted by Black people" (p. 5). Asante denies that the Africentrist philosophy is separatist. Rather it is an attempt "to center people within their own historical experiences rather than put them on the fringes of somebody else's experiences" (p. 5). Professor Maulana Karenga (1994), Afrocentric chair of the Black Studies Department at California State University– Long Beach, agrees with Asante. He, too, denies the accusations of separatism:

> You don't raise the same concern about Greek studies. You don't raise the same concern about Jewish studies. . . . The problem with that is it's catering to the idea that anything black, anything African, is somehow suspect intellectually and ethically. (p. 5)

The Asante-Karenga Africentrist camp maintains that Africentrist research views Africans and American Africans from the inside instead of from the outside as Europeans and American Europeans have done historically. Asante explicates the Africentrist enterprise as one framed by cosmological, epistemological, axiological, and aesthetic issues. This Africentrist methodology pursues a world voice distinctly African-centered in relationship to external phenomena. Asante argues that "Afrocentricity" is

> the centerpiece of human regeneration. To the degree that it is incorporated into the lives of the millions of Africans on the continent and in the Diaspora, it will become revolutionary. It is purposeful, giving a true sense of destiny based upon the facts of history and experience. The psychology of the African without Afrocentricity has become a matter of great concern. Instead of looking out from one's own center, the non-Afrocentric person operates in a manner that is negatively predictable. The person's images, symbols, lifestyles, and manners are contradictory and thereby destructive to personal and collective growth and development. Unable to call upon the power of ancestors, because one does not know them; without an ideology of heritage, because one does not respect one's own prophets; the person is like an ant trying to move a

large piece of garbage only to find it will not move. (Asante, 1988, p. 1)

The Asante Africentrists interpret Africentrism as a means by which "Africalogy" might secure its rightful place alongside other centric pluralisms without hierarchy and without seeking hegemony. In this sense, "Africalogy" is sustained by a commitment to centering the study of African phenomena and events in the particular cultural voice of the combined African people (Asante, 1990, p. 2).

University of Michigan Professor Emeritus of History and Afro-American Studies Harold Cruse contends that it is very important that an Africentrist discussion is taking place in the United States. His view is that Africentrist theory will define the impact of the African Diaspora on the twenty-first century. His position is that Africentrist theories and philosophies that are only concerned with the early beginnings of civilizations of Egypt or the best of Africa will remain merely abstractions unless scholars address what this means to individuals today:

> No one individual is going to reach this goal alone, by the way. I'm not going to do it alone. The people at Temple University, who originated the Afrocentricity concept, are not going to do it alone, either. It's going to take the thinking of our best minds to reconstruct the diasporic experience in Afrocentric terms as an approach to twenty-first century existence. . . . Now, this does not call, in my view, for an endless discussion of the impact or the meaning of Black ancient classicism. We can discuss that; it's a very important historical issue. We need the discussion for our own self-education, we need to go back and look at these ancient problems, ancient philosophies, ancient religions. I would contend that the arguments that probably went on in Ancient Egypt are the same arguments going on right here . . . today, on the questions of who is who? who was who? and who is the most important who? So, our aim is nothing new. It's ancient; it's a current concern, and it's going to the twenty-first century, the same argument about the origin of civilization. (qtd. in Vega and Greene, 1993, p. 14)

Though the argument about the origin of civilization is not new, it certainly has expanded greatly since the creation-versus-evolution debates. As mentioned, countless approaches to the origin of humankind are in full discussion, many of which are African-focused. Therefore, such monolithic criticism of Africentrist philosophies and theories is highly inaccurate and leads to unfair, biased, and unsound criticism. It becomes especially problematic as it relates to Africentricity in the public schools. For example, the African-centered curriculum in Detroit Academies is completely different from the African American Immersion Academies in Milwaukee, which is different from other Africentrist programs. It is purely inaccurate and highly unethical to present a single criticism of these programs as they are inherently different.

Summary

As stated earlier, this work is predicated on the fact that education can play a most crucial role in providing or not providing opportunities for social and individual mobility. The all-male academy movement presents a unique opportunity to analyze the structure of schooling and to examine the varying structures of power and power relations which exist at its very crux. It is not the domination of the "powers that be" (i.e., civic and political organizations) that is of paramount concern here. Rather, it is most important to discuss the concepts of power, spirit, strength, and determination resounding among American African educators and community leaders who refused to completely abandon plans for schools and programs for American African males even after sanctions by school districts, complaints from civic organizations, and even mandates from Federal courts forbade their opening.

The power that I am discussing is akin to that Seth Kreisberg (1992) discusses. He describes the issue of power and control of decision making as the ability to threaten and, if need be, apply severe sanctions. Lasswell and Kaplan explain as follows:

Power is a form of influence in which the effect on policy is enforced or expected to be enforced by relatively severe sanctions. Power is participation in the making of decisions: G has power over H with respect to the values K if G participates in the making of decisions affecting the K-policies of H. . . . A decision is a policy involving severe sanctions (deprivations).

. . . The definition of power in terms of decision making adds an important element to "the production of intended effects on other persons"—namely, the availability of sanctions when the intended effects are not forthcoming. (qtd. in Kreisberg, 1992, p. 41)

This definition of power and sanctions directly parallels the plight of the all-male academy movement and other schools and programs for American African males. This power, which influences and affects policy as well as imposes sanctions, denied all-male academies even the slightest chance to educate Black males.

Although several schools and programs throughout the country do operate under some variation of the initially proposed all-male academy tenets, because of "power(s) that be"—including the United States Federal Court, the American Civil Liberties Union, the National Association for the Advancement of Colored People, and the National Organization of Women's Education and Defense Fund—absolutely none were "permitted" to operate fully based on three of the most important tenets recommended by the experts in education and on Black male culture. These tenets—early intervention with the infusion of American African male role models, gender separation, and African-centered curriculum—were features identified early on as three of the most effective paradigm changes needed in public education for American African males to achieve liberation, especially in light of their miseducation and their often irreversible environmental carnage. However, they became three of the most challenged issues by opponents of the all-male schools.

Lasswell and Kaplan view power as the ability to create intended effects on other people. This notion of intentionality and linear cause-and-effect are central to their conception of power, as it is the fundamental line between power and imposition. Undergirding their definition is a model of community characterized by inherent conflict and competition for control over decision making. Bierstadt points out that while indeed there exists a distinction between power and influence, there is also a subtle distinction between the use of sanctions and the threat of sanctions:

Influence is persuasive whereas power is coercive. We submit voluntarily to influence but power requires our submission.

. . . Power is not force and power is not authority, but it is intimately related to both. (1) Power is latent force; (2) force is manifest power, and (3) authority is institutionalized power. . . . Force means the production of an effect, an alteration in movement or action that overcomes resistance. . . . In the sociological sense, where it is synonymous with coercion, it compels a change in the course of action of an individual or a group against the wishes of the individual or the group. It means the application of sanctions when they are not willingly received. Only groups that have power can threaten to use force, and the threat itself is power. . . . Without power there is no organization and without power there is no order. (qtd. in Kreisberg, 1992, p. 41)

It is precisely this underlying dominant conception of power which underpins the discourses on power discussed further in this work.

3

In the Midst of Storm:
A Description of Models

Alternative schools and educational programs designed specifically to meet the needs of American African males are relatively new; many of these programs are school-based, but some are merely school-linked. They have been implemented largely as a grassroots effort to intercede in the increasing demise of young American African males. These schools and programs are designed in a number of ways. Some models are entire schools; some are single classes within the schools; others are pull-out programs, before- and after-school programs, mentoring and tutoring programs, and male-development programs. The schools and programs target different age groups from preschool to high school (Ascher, 1992).

Carol Ascher (1991) points out that all of the alternative schools and educational programs focus on helping American African male youth develop productive behaviors and values by bringing them into contact with American African male adults. The following are common characteristics of the schools and programs: identity/self-esteem building, academic values and skills, parent and community strengthening, transition to manhood, and safe havens.

These features have been deemed essential strategies for educating American African males. Johnson and Watson (1993) indicate that the features are a part of a proactive pedagogy to combat negative media stereotypes of American African males. Because

the public image of American African males is often harsh and un-
attractive, the self-image of American African males has been ex-
tinguished. Further, the negative images and stereotyping of
American African males affect the decision making of teachers,
principals, police, judges, and other authority figures. Ascher
(1991) identifies five specific effects of the devaluation of American
African males as:

> (1) American African males have a shorter life span than any
> other group in the United States, due to a disproportionate
> vulnerability to disease and homicide; (2) structural changes
> in labor market and racially discriminatory hiring practices
> create high unemployment among American African men,
> wide gaps between the earnings of American African and
> American European men, and a disproportionate number of
> American African men living in poverty; (3) dysfunctional so-
> ciopsychological conditions include a number of female-
> headed families, a lack of positive male role models, intra-
> racial crime, and low levels of educational attainment; (4) the
> internalized negative self-image and the negative attitudes of
> authority figures result in the disproportionate involvement
> of American African males with the criminal justice system;
> and (5) the location of drug markets within American African
> communities results in an increase in violence and drug
> abuse. All-male schools and programs are designed to prevent
> American African males from falling prey to the aforemen-
> tioned atrocities and to provide a quality educational experi-
> ence that will hopefully lead to productive citizenship. (p. 10)

There are a host of schools and programs designed for American
African males. Many of these schools and programs employ pedagogy and techniques especially targeted to insure that American
African males are offered optimal learning opportunities. This
work identifies thirty schools and programs designed to educate
Black males (see chapter 4 and appendix B for additional descriptions). The schools and programs can be divided into five catego-
ries: (1) whole male schools, (2) evolving male schools, (3) single-
gender classes, (4) school-affiliated male programs, and (5) community-based male programs.

Whole Male Schools

Despite legal challenges, at least three schools operate with overwhelmingly American African male student populations. The three whole male schools are Malcolm X African-Centered Academy, Detroit; Marcus Garvey African-Centered Academy, Detroit; and Paul Robeson African-Centered Academy, Detroit.

The Detroit Public Schools is the national model for whole male schools, as this was the first public district to set up a whole-male-school approach. On 22 August 1991, only four days before the opening of Malcolm X, Marcus Garvey, and Paul Robeson Academies, the ACLU and NOW filed suit on behalf of three American African women who alleged that the creation of the all-male academies discriminated against their daughters. On 31 August 1991, federal judge George Woods granted the injunction and ordered the Detroit Public School Board to arrange a compromise that would not discriminate against females. In compliance with the court order, the Detroit School Board agreed to reopen admission to the academies and to admit females into the schools, which were to be called "African-Centered" Academies. The district voted to waive the right to an appeal (Watson and Smitherman, 1992).

The Detroit African-centered academies—Malcolm X, Marcus Garvey, and Paul Robeson—were founded as an African-centered program stressing multicultural, humanistic, and futuristic education. Students at the academies, grades K–8, are expected to develop academic excellence, ethnic awareness and pride, and high self-esteem. The staff is committed to the goal of providing a quality education to all students. While the Academy environment is highly disciplined, it is nurturing and friendly. Although, the 1991 federal decision ruled that Detroit Public Schools could not run an all-male academy, the District currently operates three academies with an enrollment of nearly 90 percent American African males (Detroit Public Schools, 1993).

Evolving Male Schools

The evolving male schools manage a heterogeneous student population, with equal numbers of males and females. Two of the schools were proposed as whole male schools; however, because of legal challenges, they now operate within the school district with an emphasis on African and American African history and culture. These relatively new schools are currently conducting research and making plans to implement specific strategies for educating Black males and females, including rites of passage and academic enrichment. The three evolving male schools are Dr. Martin Luther King Jr. African American Immersion Academy, Milwaukee; Malcolm X African American Immersion School, Milwaukee; and Ujamma Institute–Medgar Evers College, New York.

In the Milwaukee public schools, the Dr. Martin Luther King Jr. African American Immersion Academy and the Malcolm X African Immersion School (formerly Robert L. Fulton Middle School) evolved as a result of a failed initiative for a whole male school. The schools were designed to eliminate the institutional and attitudinal influences that impede the academic success of American African males. However, due to fear of legal challenges, the schools now admit American African female students as well (Ascher, 1992). The goal of the schools is to prepare all students to live, learn, and work in a culturally diverse society and to prevent the increase of adverse statistics that are largely represented by American African males in the school district (Leake and Leake, 1992). However, the school is designing a specialized program for Black males.

The Ujamaa Institute–Medgar Evers College was designed as an experimental high school run collaboratively by the New York City Board of Education and Medgar Evers College in Brooklyn. Opened in September 1994, the institute manages a heterogeneous student population. The state-required curriculum is used in addition to a multicultural curriculum emphasizing African and American African history and culture. The institute includes special instruction and teaching styles for all of its students, including American African males (Ascher, 1991, p 29).

Single-Gender Classes

Single-gender classes allow American African males unique schooling opportunities. Such classes have been a successful technique for parents, school administrators, and other school people to avoid civil rights discrimination suits. There are six public schools with single-gender classes for some of their American African males: (1) Coldstream Elementary School, Baltimore; (2) Robert Coleman Elementary School, Baltimore; (3) George G. Kelson Elementary School, Baltimore; (4) Matthew A. Henson Elementary School, Baltimore; (5) Pine Villa Elementary School, Dade County; and (6) Stanton Elementary School, Washington, D.C.

The Baltimore City Public Schools (BCPS) and Washington, D.C., Public System are two major urban systems that have successfully implemented single-gender classes, with a special emphasis on the American African male. Since the 1989–90 school year, these BCPS elementary schools have created and maintained all-male classes taught by American African male teachers (Holland, 1992). The all-male class at Matthew A. Henson Elementary School in Baltimore is four years old. The class was established to treat "the main problems the boys face: low self-esteem and lack of good role models" (qtd. in Ascher, 1992, p. 778). The class, which is taught by an American African male, began with second graders; students and teacher stay together as the students are promoted (Ascher, 1992).

The all-male classes at Robert Coleman Elementary School, Coldstream Park Elementary, George G. Kelson Elementary, and Stanton Elementary are also four years old. These classes are designed to help the boys catch up with the girls. The boys tend to come from needy, single-parent homes. The class aims to improve their self-esteem and give them a positive male teacher as role model.

The Pine Villa Elementary School–At Risk Male Class services American African students who come from low-income, female-headed families, with a large proportion on federal assistance and welfare. Two all-male classrooms, one kindergarten and one first grade, were implemented during the 1987–88 school year. The program focused on attendance, academic achievement, dyads, gentlemen's social graces, and appropriate behavior for school life. Placed in a "buddy system," students learn effective ways of dealing with confrontation and practice the concept of "brother's keeper" (qtd. in Ascher, p. 22).

Virtually all of the existing schools designed to intervene in the demise of American African male youth incorporate some outreach initiative that includes mentoring, tutoring, and other activities involving the local community, churches, fraternities, colleges and universities, and civic and social organizations. The community outreach component has been deemed an invaluable ingredient in educating American African males in the alternative education models.

School-Affiliated Programs

School-affiliated programs exist as an outreach component to augment the education of Black males at existing schools. The programs have established partnerships with individual schools and/or entire school districts in the fight to educate Black males. Some of these programs operate with alternative schools for Black males; others focus on tapping into schools with high American African male populations which are not specially designed for teaching Black males. There are eleven school-affiliated programs: (1) East End Neighborhood House, Cleveland; (2) Fulton Academics and Athletic Magnet, San Diego; (3) The HAWK Project, Sacramento; (4) Wake County Public Schools Helping Hands Project, Raleigh, North Carolina; (5) Inroads/Wisconsin Inc., Milwaukee; (6) Man to Man, Detroit; (7) Manhood Incorporated, Detroit, (8) "My Brother's Keeper" Program, East Lansing; (9) Project 2000, Baltimore; (10) "Save A Star" Male Leadership Development, Detroit; and (11) Woodward Elementary School "Star" Mentoring Program, Detroit.

The East End Neighborhood House conducts an Africentric Rites of Passage Program with American African students in two East Cleveland public schools. The program services twenty-five males and twenty-five females at three sites: fifth and sixth graders at in the Focus/Scope Primary Magnet School and seventh and eighth graders in Kirk Middle School. The programs take place two afternoons a week after school and from 9–12 on Saturdays (Ascher, 1991, p. 17).

Fulton Academics and Athletics has a full-time American African male student advocate who meets weekly with the school's American African male students by classroom groups. The program offers training in social skills, as well as a curriculum reflecting African and American African culture and history. The program provides positive role models, mentors, individual and group counseling, tutorial services, and a support network of American African males. Staff development at the school focuses on providing teachers with information on learning styles and other issues that enhance the development of American African male students (Ascher, 1991, p. 19).

The HAWK program was initiated at Grant Union High School, Sacramento, in conjunction with the Institute for the Advanced Study of Black Family, Life, and Culture, Oakland, in the fall of 1988, with the primary goal of increasing male responsibility in teenage pregnancy. The program uses African and American African history and African rituals to develop "competent, confident, and conscious African American men," and can serve to prevent problems with drugs, gangs, low aspirations, or academic failure. At Grant Union, students begin the HAWK program in the ninth grade and are enrolled through the twelfth grade. The participants attend two pull-out classes as well as two after-school classes each month. The program attempts to develop in each young man:

(1) something which he does exceptionally well (competence); (2) a belief that whatever the task, he can be successful at it (confidence); (3) an awareness of the historical greatness of African and African- American men and their personal responsibility to the future continuation of that greatness (consciousness). (Ascher, 1991, p. 27)

The School/Community Helping Hands Project, Wake County Public Schools, Raleigh, North Carolina, matches American African role models, first from the school system and then from the community, with young American African males in grades 3–8. Activities and strategies are targeted toward four areas: self-esteem, school achievement, interpersonal relations, and leadership development. Helping Hands embraces the concept that "all students can learn and become productive citizens in society." It attempts to engage the American African male child, who has consistently lagged behind in school achievement, to fully access educational opportunities (Wake County Public School System, 1993).

The Inroads Youth leadership Academy, an attempt by Inroads/ Wisconsin to help develop young American African males into productive, contributing members of the corporate world, has been in operation since 1990. The program targets third-, fourth-, and fifth-grade male students to improve their self-concept and decision-making skills. The program is voluntary; however, school principals do recommend some students. The program offers after-school and Saturday classes based on a curriculum designed to build both academic and personal skills (Ascher, 1991, p. 20).

"Man To Man" is a mentoring, male-bonding program through which students at Detroit's Paul Robeson African Centered Academy are mentored by volunteers representing a variety of backgrounds and professions, including police officers, custodial personnel, teachers, physicians, and others. The volunteers "receive" the American African male students on Wednesday from 4–6 P.M. The males are formally greeted by the adult mentors and are all welcomed with the "Paul Robeson" handshake, a firm handshake where the boys and adult males engage in eye to eye contact. At 6 P.M., the members meet with community people to convene a Black "think tank" to discuss any issues about schooling and community that concerned community citizens wish to address (R. Johnson, personal communication, December 1993).

Manhood Incorporated is a component of the Detroit Marcus Garvey African Centered Academy. The mentor group consists of all-male parents and caregivers for the students at Marcus Garvey. On Tuesday and Thursday afternoons, the parents meet with students to provide mentoring, including tutorial services. Male-bonding activities include discussions on male-related issues, such as self-respect, academic achievement, and community responsibility. The goal of the program is to ensure that all male students, especially those with absent male models, are exposed to positive American African male models (H. Hambrick, personal communication, December 1993).

"My Brother's Keeper" Program is a partnership effort whereby American African students from Michigan State University serve as tutors, role models, and mentors for students at the Malcolm X Academy. Major interaction with the students at Malcolm X Academy involves hosting the students several times per year on the Michigan State University campus, including a summer retreat. A goal of this program is to introduce American African male youth early on to the college environment to better prepare American African youth and their parents for college life and expectations ("My Brother's Keeper" Program, 1991).

In June 1990, the Center for Educating African-American Males (CEAAM) was founded at Morgan State University. In association with the School of Education and Urban Studies, the primary goal is to develop and implement programs aimed at improving the rate of academic success of American African male students in the Baltimore Public City Schools. One program adopted by CEAAM is Project 2000. Project 2000 recruits and trains adult male volunteers, particularly American African males, to serve as teacher assistants in classrooms from kindergarten through third grade. In general, the aim of these programs is to tap the potential of American African youth, inoculating them against hostile forces existing in their environment, which often lead to their eradication. Project 2000 implements programs in public schools in Baltimore; Washington, D.C., Dade County, Miami; Paterson, N.J.; Kirkwood, Missouri; Annapolis; and in an independent school in Chicago. Most of these programs are sponsored by community efforts; however, Project 2000—New Brunswick is the only fully corporate model where all volunteers are corporate employees and are given release-time from work to participate. Kirkwood is the only suburban model, while Baltimore and Newark are the only two university-sponsored models (*Project 2000 Trainer's Manual*, 1991, p. 3).

"Save A Star" Male Leadership Development Preventative Drop Out Program at Monnier Elementary School began in January 1987 in response to the alarming number of males in grades 3–5 who were being referred to the administration for disciplinary action, and who were often excluded from classes and suspended from school. Male students whose citizenship and academic achievement are below average and show signs of being potential drop-outs begin meeting with a male physical education teacher, a female counselor, and a female social worker once a week. Meetings involve activities developing positive American African male identity, helping the student learn conflict resolution, improving his self-esteem, building internal motivation for behavior and academic success, and developing career goals. Several times a month, students are also exposed to male role models "who beat the odds." In addition, Monnier staff voluntarily tutor these boys in reading, math, spelling, science, computer math, and citizenship after school from 3–4 P.M., on Monday through Thursday. Finally, parents are provided with information and training to assist them in more effectively rearing their sons (Ascher, 1991, p. 22). Ascher reports that the results of the program have already been impressive. Since January 1988, no males have been suspended from Monnier School. There has also been a decrease in males referred to the office for disciplinary action, the grade-point average of boys in the program improved by "C" or better in language arts and math, and male students have shown "an improved attitude about the meaning and purpose of school" (Ascher, 1991, p. 22).

The "Star" Mentoring Program is an after-school program at Woodward Elementary School in Detroit. Founded by former principal Dr. Clifford Watson, Judith Jackson, and Debra Walls, the aim of the program is to provide young Black boys with positive male mentors from the Detroit community. The program serves American African students in grades 3–5 and offers tutorial services and mentoring. Black males from Black Men, Inc., and from a local Detroit Armory volunteer serve as mentors for the program (J. Jackson, personal communication, May 1994).

Community-Based Programs

Community-based programs are those mentoring, male role-modeling, tutorial, and self-esteem programs designed by civic groups, churches, fraternities, and other community organizations as a proactive community stance against the oppression of American African males. Organizations ranked American African males high on their list of priorities to join the fight to save American African males. The seven community-based programs are (1) Black Male College Explorers Program–A&M College, Tallahassee; (2) Children of the Sun/Tampa Urban League, Tampa; (3) Concerned Black Men, Inc., Washington, D.C.; (4) Morehouse Mentoring Program, Atlanta; (5) Project Alpha, Baltimore; (6) RAAMUS Academy, Cincinnati; and (7) Toussaint Institute Fund, Inc., New York.

The Black Male College Explorers program in Tallahassee addresses the problem of low college attendance among Black males and their high postsecondary dropout rate. Sponsored by A&M College, Florida's only public historically Black college, the program says to American African males, "if you get your act together, we will get you into college and keep you there." The program targets students in ninth through twelfth grades, but students begin in the eighth grade so that they can have four to five years of a six-week summer intervention program prior to attending the college of their choice (Ascher, 1991, p. 28).

The Children of the Sun and the Greater Tampa Urban League

created a fourteen-week after-school program based on addressing five risk factors among American African males: (1) crime and delinquency, (2) health and longevity, (3) education, (4) economic development, and (5) family and community life. The program serves American African youth from ten to eighteen years of age with a four-part intervention. First, a lecture is given by an American African physician, focusing on the promotion of health and prevention of disease, and including physical examinations. Second, students take a fourteen-week course that reinforces health issues while focusing on American African culture, history, heritage, and values. In this course, three values are stressed: (a) respect for self, family, elders, and community; (b) responsibility to self, sexuality, family, and community; and (c) self-development in the areas of education, health, economic development, and family life. The third intervention includes a "rites of passage" program in which the graduates participate. The fourth and final intervention links the American African male with a mentor (Ascher, 1991, p. 26).

Concerned Black Men, Inc., implemented Project 2000, named after the class of the year 2000, for students who entered the third grade in 1990–91. The premise is that young American African males need male models of success if they are to avoid reproducing the negative images all around them. The program includes mentoring seminars on topics such as self-esteem, and projects designed to enhance students' self-esteem. The group has an annual Youth Recognition Awards Banquet, a Martin Luther King Jr. Oratory Contest, and an African American History Bee (Ascher, 1991, p. 30).

The Morehouse Mentoring Program at Morehouse College, Atlanta, currently operates under the Office of Community Service and provides mentoring activities undertaken by Morehouse College students for precollegiate male students. The program is based on the Morehouse College tradition of developing men who will lead lives of leadership and service, and who will have a positive impact on society (*Office of Community Service* brochure, 1993).

Alpha Phi Alpha Fraternity, Inc., the first American African Greek-letter fraternity, created Project Alpha as a community intervention program for American African males. Project Alpha is a national component of all active Alpha Phi Alpha Chapters. The goal is to expose American African male teens to adult male models, emphasizing sexual responsibility. The Project Alpha conference, hosted by individual chapters nationwide, includes seminars, workshops, and presentations which address the issue of male responsibility in teen pregnancy. Seminars often include moral/religious, health awareness, and legality components.

Another outreach program is the RAAMUS Academy (Responsible African American Men United in Spirit), in Cincinnati, Ohio. The RAAMUS Academy is an after-school education and "reeducation" program for young American African males ages 9 to 14. This program uses "edu-tainment," that is the process of using entertainment and fun in order to inspire, excite, and educate young American African males about cultural awareness and academic achievement (*RAAMUS Academy Handbook*, 1991).

The Toussaint Institute Fund, Inc., contends that American African males are unruly, poor students in public schools because the general tone of the school, including its low expectations for them, encourages such behavior. The organization seeks American African, low-income, elementary boys who are experiencing repeated failure in public schools. The Toussaint Institute provides these Black males with 90 percent of the funds necessary to attend a historically Black independent college of their choice. As with most of the schools and programs, the paramount goal is to empower Black males as individuals and as successful, productive, responsible members of communities which need their contributions in order to survive.

4

The New Program: Approaches to Teaching Black Males

Black children: they are the future and hope of Black America. Our struggle to develop their potential must begin with rescuing them from the victimization of the American miseducational system.

—Geneva Smitherman, 1981, p.11

The New Program—alternative schools and programs for Black males—was designed to rescue American African males from a "miseducational system" which has continually failed them. This chapter recounts six interviews with school administrators and program directors: (1) Dr. Clifford Watson, principal and founder, Malcolm X African-Centered Academy, Detroit; (2) Ray Johnson, principal, Paul Robeson African-Centered Academy, Detroit; (3) Josephine Hill, program coordinator, Malcolm X African American Immersion Academy, Milwaukee; (4) Anita Sparks, program coordinator, Dr. Martin Luther King Jr. African American Immersion Academy, Milwaukee; (5) Pryce Baldwin Jr., project manager, Helping Hands Project, Wake County Public Schools, Raleigh, North Carolina; (6) Dr. Spencer Holland, founder and director,

Project 2000, Center for Educating African American Males, Morgan State University, Baltimore.

This chapter describes these six alternative schools and programs designed for Black males as they seek to eradicate the historical instructional paradigm leading to the miseducation of Black males. Parents, teachers, and researchers, who work in the New Program for American African males have recommended a host of curriculum strategies, teaching methods, and socialization processes essential in ensuring responsible and effective teaching for Black males (see appendix A). This chapter allows administrators and directors to detail these strategies, methods, and male-development processes employed in the New Program.

"By Any Means Necessary"

In the Warrendale community, on the Detroit Westside, a flag waves atop a two-story brick school building. No, it is not the typical red, white, and blue flag that one might expect to adorn public schools, public offices, and federal buildings. Rather, this flag is red, black, and green. These colors represent the spirit of Africaneity. The red represents the blood of slain African ancestors; the green symbolizes the continent of Africa; and the black represents all peoples of African descent. This flag epitomizes the major emphasis of the Detroit Malcolm X African-Centered Academy. Dr. Clifford Watson, principal and founder, explains:

> What you see in our school are those images that are pertinent to Black children, to raise their self-esteem to make them believe in themselves. When they walk out and see the tri-colored flag flying over the building, they say, "That's our flag." So then they want to come to school. They want to learn. (Interview, 1993)

About twelve years ago, Dr. Watson envisioned a school in Detroit for Black males. After considerable contemplation and agonizing, Dr. Watson formally proposed the all-male academy idea to the Detroit Public School Board of Education in 1990. Basically, two shocking statistics fueled his desire to implement an all-male school: (1) the leading cause of death for American African males ages 15–24 is homicide, and (2) more than 50 percent of Black males were dropping out of school—mentally and physically—at early ages. The all-male academy was an attempt to do something about the drastic situation for urban Black males. The Board enthusiastically accepted the proposal and charged Dr. Watson and a Male Academy Task Force to develop implementation strategies.

The name Malcolm X was chosen by the school community because of Malcolm X's legacy, which parallels the plight and struggle of many Black males today. Dr. Watson explained that just as Malcolm X epitomized Black Nationalism from a practical perspective, he evolved to embrace the good in all races. And so, a goal of the Malcolm X Academy became to provide academic and social support for Black males in the local Detroit community and to send a message to the entire national American African community that a safe, educational environment must be created for Black males if they are to be sheltered from the hostile forces of the streets and protected from historical inequality within the public school.

In the design of the all-male academy, Dr. Watson and the task force maintained that in order to address Black male underachievement, preventive strategies were needed at the elementary-school level because Black males began to drop out mentally as early as third grade. Another factor considered in the development of the program was that many Black males grow up not learning how to treat Black women—or themselves, for that matter. As a result of this ill socialization, many Black boys grow up to abuse and disrespect women and themselves. The rationale for the academy was to address this prospective problem early on with Black boys and to teach them self-respect and appropriate approaches to treating other people, especially Black women. Given that 70 percent or more of urban households are headed by women, Black boys were not encountering positive Black male role models. Consequently, they grow up repeating many of the negative behaviors they see on the streets. The task force conjectured that the academy might be a perfect way to provide Black males with positive role models who would engage in appropriate male-bonding activities and conscientious development.

After planning for nearly a year to open the all-male academy, the Detroit Public Schools found themselves faced with a legal controversy (see preface). Consequently, three would-be academies— Malcolm X, Marcus Garvey, and Paul Robeson—opened on September 1991 as African-Centered Academies. Though Dr. Watson's dream of implementing an all-male academy was temporarily suspended, the male academy became Malcolm X African-Centered Academy, K–8. Of its 480 students, 417 are Black males, and 76 are Black females. As well as maintaining a high population of American African males, the program heavily recruits Black male teachers and paraprofessionals. In fact, out of the seventeen teachers and staff, twelve are American African males, two are American European males, five are American African females, and two are American European females.

One objective of the New Program is to establish a safe haven for American African males to protect them from the often-hostile inner-city environment. The mission statement of Detroit's Malcolm X African-Centered Academy speaks to the general philosophy, desired campus climate, and the faculty and staff attitudes generated in most of these schools and programs:

> The Malcolm X Academy was founded as an African-Centered program, stressing multicultural, humanistic, and futuristic education. Students at the Academy will be expected to develop academic excellence, ethnic awareness and pride, and high self-esteem. The staff, trained in addressing the needs of urban youth, is committed to the goal of providing a quality education to all students. The environment of the Malcolm X Academy will be disciplined, but nurturing and friendly. (Detroit Public Schools, 1993, p. 3)

To achieve the goal of providing students with a "multicultural, humanistic, and futuristic" educational experience, Malcolm X adopted the Africentrist theory of Molefi Asante and Maulana Karenga. This Africentrist camp views African people as agents of their historical experience, social construction, and change, rather than mere objects surviving on the fringes of Europe, a common oppressor. The hallways and classrooms at Malcolm X Academy are fully embellished with representations of African and American African culture and heritage. Pictures, paintings, sculptures, kente cloth, poems, and other artifacts reflect the cultures of African and American African civilizations. As a part of the Africentrist program, Dr. Watson explains that these strategies assist in building student self-confidence and self-esteem and rightfully repudiate the myth of Africa as the "heart of darkness." The basis for this visual display of Africanaeity is that many American African students attend schools which are predominantly Black, yet in these schools they only see images of Europeans and American Europeans. These are often historical figures who greatly contributed to the oppression of peoples of African descent. Dr. Watson asks:

Why, when you look at the walls in the public schools, do you only see George Washington, a slave owner. Why are there no positive images of Black people? Where is Malcolm X, Marcus Garvey, Mary McLeod Bethune, and other Black leaders? (Interview, 1993)

Not only is there a visual connection to Africanaeity at Malcolm X Academy, there is an entire emphasis in the curriculum. Dr. Watson explains that the required curriculum as mandated by Michigan Public Act 25—to teach children world studies, art, science, reading, math, and writing—is being satisfied beyond requirements. However, the disciplines are taught from an African perspective. Central to the success of teaching this Africentrist curriculum are the faculty and staff. Dr. Watson deems the visibility of Black male role models within the classroom essential in the education of the students. He believes that the faculty and staff must be well trained to address the special needs of urban males if they are to work in such an environment. The teachers are educated so that they can accurately and confidently instruct their classes from an African perspective. Dr. Watson says that at Malcolm X Academy teachers must be grounded in the philosophy of African-centered education, and that students, for the most part, must have teachers who look like them. He declares, "If the teachers are not committed to African-centered education, then I get rid of them, be they Black or White" (Interview, 1993).

It is evident that the chief priority of Malcolm X Academy is its students. The Detroit students are selected on a bell-curve, that is, one-third high performance, one-third middle performance, and one-third low performance. Illustrative of the demand for quality education in Detroit, parents have their children on a two-year waiting list for kindergarten. Most are not expected to be admitted before third or fourth grade. Black males are provided a rites-of-passage program whereby male teachers and adult and young adult community volunteers serve as mentors, tutors, and male friends to the Black boys. This "brother to brother" interaction aims to foster a sense of communal ties. Additionally, students participate in after-school and Saturday programs on an eleven-month academic calendar. In addition, parents are required to volunteer a minimum of three hours per month. French, Ki-Swahili, and Spanish are taught, beginning in kindergarten.

The spirit of academic excellence, communal responsibility, and hope for the uplifting of Black peoples is best delivered through the Malcolm X Academy Pledge. The pledge is performed daily by the students and staff and at special ceremonies and events. In resounding voices with heads held high, in unison they declare:

> We, at the Malcolm X Academy
> will strive for excellence
> in our quest to be the best.
> We'll rise above every challenge
> with our heads held high.
> We'll always keep the faith
> when others say die.
> March on till victory
> is ours: AMANDLA!!
> —Vincent Edgecombe

"On A Mission"

Paul Robeson African-Centered Academy began out of the Detroit All-Male Academy Initiative. Principal Ray Johnson was an administrator at Cooper Middle School and had for years been involved with helping to hold onto young Black boys. He started a program called "Man to Man" about twelve years ago specifically to encourage Black boys to stay in school. As director of a gifted-and-talented program in Detroit, he observed that eighth-grade males were dropping out, while the remaining ones were not completing the program. Principal Johnson targeted the eighth-grade males and invited some men to volunteer for mentoring. He said:

> In August, I called about ten of my corporate friends and we talked about what we needed to do to save our Black males.

"Listen, we've got to have a man-to-man talk," I said.

"Well what do you need us to do Ray?" they asked.

Young Black males need to see you, hear you, touch you, smell you. They need to know what it is to be male because I'm finding that they're just not respecting themselves or others, and they lack the level of motivation to be successful. (Interview, 1993)

Johnson successfully recruited about ten brothers, who came in once a week to sit down and spend time with Black males. The men organized group sessions with the Black boys on decision-making and other interpersonal skills, academic planning, conflict resolution, and goal-setting skills. Johnson began to see changes in the boys' attitudes, grades, and behaviors. Upon his transfer to an elementary school, Johnson moved the "Man to Man" program and modified it for the elementary school. Johnson observed that most mentoring programs for Black males targeted middle- and high-school students, but few addressed the needs of Black males at the elementary grades. Because of Johnson's initiative and visible role in mentoring Black males in Detroit, the Detroit Board of Education heavily courted him as a possible head of one of the three experimental all-male academies.

The board charged Johnson and a Male Academy Task Force to develop operational strategies for a school for males which incorporated a regularized mentoring program with over one hundred Black male volunteers. Johnson, the precursor, called the all-male school "Paul Robeson Academy." Johnson selected more than just a name, but an image that the students, staff, and community could be proud of. For Johnson, Paul Robeson represents everything the academy stood for. Robeson was an academic scholar, a man of principle, a world-class leader who excelled at everything from sports to oratory. He was the first collegian ever to win the National Debate Championship and he won two years in a row. He was an All-American in football, baseball, and track, and even played professional football. Robeson attended Columbia Law School, earned a law degree, and was a noted playwright. Johnson expressed his admiration for Robeson:

Paul Robeson was the true Renaissance man as they call it. But I think I was most impressed with his stand for Africa. He created the African World Council way back in the early thirties. And when you read his books and hear his speeches, if you close your eyes, you would think it was Malcolm X or Martin speaking. Yet, he predated all of them. And then the other striking thing was his amazing ability to captivate audiences all over the world. When I took our staff on retreat, I met a gentleman who had met Paul Robeson in Czechoslovakia. He told me how Robeson sang in their language and made them cry, and then he spoke of liberation in their language. He wrote letters in Chinese, he communicated with folks in Japanese, he had acquired knowledge of about twenty languages, and when the government attempted to silence his voice for speaking out against injustice against Americans and people around the world, he refused to do so. So when I selected Paul Robeson, I thought about a model for our young Black males. I wanted them to have a model, and image with that level of commitment to humanity. (Interview, 1993)

The board asked, "Well where will you start?" Johnson explained:

I had eight classrooms in the basement of the elementary school that were not being used. A couple were just used for storage. Some of that stuff had been stored for over twenty years, so we had to get all of that out of there. We built an office out of one of the classrooms down there and installed wires and the whole works, which was an incredible amount of work that we had to do. I drew up the plans because the architect for this building was not exactly a friend to this whole project. He was stonewalling it. So I went to some tradesmen and spent eight hours learning how to draw plans for an office, because that's what was holding up renovation of the building. I was able to develop a plan and submit it under the name of a guy who I knew was on vacation. I don't think that guy to this day knew that it was not the guy who on vacation that drew those plans up, but we knew we only had thirty days before we were to open the school. (Interview, 1993)

The school became a school within a school, the regular elementary school and the Paul Robeson All-Male Academy. The school campus had two different staffs, two different student bodies, two different parent groups, and one principal. Prior to opening for the school year, Johnson included some of the regular elementary-school staff members in the planning, and included many of the students from the elementary school in the program in order to avoid an elitist or antagonistic situation right at the heart of the school. From his training and experience with staff development, Johnson was able to select a staff who showed commitment, competence, and yet confidence to "carry out the mission" of the Academy. Johnson said:

> After looking at their ability, I had what I call a "Mission Quotient," and I tried to evaluate their sense of mission. I've been very successful in identifying folks that have an uncommon level of commitment. If staff demonstrated anything less than an extraordinary sense of mission about what we do, we wouldn't be able to do it. So we were able to gather a very talented group of folks and put together a curriculum for the program. It was very difficult in the beginning because we were being sued by the National Organization of Women and the American Civil Liberties Union. We didn't have a budget for our school downstairs, the Male Academy. There were grievances filed against me by both the administrative unit and the Detroit Federation of Teachers because their claim was that I couldn't operate a school within a school. And I couldn't serve as the principal for two schools at the same time. So there was this debate as to the legitimacy and legality of the all-male program to begin with. (Interview, 1993)

Johnson and the task force promised the community that if they hosted the school for one year, the school would find a new building and would be able to move out. They promised that upon vacating the school they would leave it in better condition. A goal of the academy was that wherever they moved, they would build up that school, area, and community. The program was fortunate enough to find another building in the general area.

Though the original concept of the all-male academy was severely altered, the Paul Robeson African-Centered Academy, pre-K–4, has strived to provide an uncompromised level of commitment to American African males and to the Detroit community. Sixty-eight percent of the students are at poverty level or below and come from the lower east side of Detroit. Students are selected by a lottery process—random selection—and once selected, they and their parents go before an admissions committee made up of parents, staff members, and members of the community. Essentially the interviews are to clarify the mission of the academy with parents and students, and to ensure that they are willing to make a commitment to participating in this learning environment.

The academy organizes an entrepreneurial program whereby youngsters take pilot training in grade four. At age nine, the students, the youngest group in the country to do so, take pilot training, aviation, and aeronautics. The students will soon navigate a cross-country flight and consequently earn their piloting license. The entrepreneurial program is one that is headed by one of the Spanish teachers. The students learn about the stock market, stock exchange, and real estate investments. Other Paul Robeson Academy programs include acquiring homes to offer students opportunities to run the companies that will renovate the homes, including leasing them and monitoring the real estate investments and values. Students go through economic "rites of passage," and by the time they go to middle and high school, they have acquired capitol to invest in businesses of their choice along with scholarships for college.

To establish a sense of community, Paul Robeson students are required to wear uniforms. The idea is to create a unified campus climate, build self-esteem, and eliminate peer jealousy and envy. The uniforms display the school emblem and campus theme, "On A Mission." Principal Johnson maintains that by wearing uniforms American African males will be taught to focus on an individual's actions, character, and his inner being, not merely his outward appearance. To visually express their sense of unity and school morale, Paul Robeson faculty and staff members frequently wear jackets and tee shirts with the Academy theme.

A "rites of passage" model is employed as a critical component of Paul Robeson Academy. In rites of passage, American African men serve as mentors to American African boys. Critical to this socialization process for American African boys is the opportunity to discuss with the American African men the cumbersome issues (e.g. economics, relationships, etc.) involved in bringing boys to manhood. They help the boys by sharing their experiences and by providing support, encouragement, and guidance. An Africentrist Rites-of-Passage model is preferred and used in the Paul Robeson

Academy. The Africentrist rites-of-passage model promotes positive development of American African males, while simultaneously instilling a sense of communalism and addressing the exceptional needs of American African males by teaching them the concept of social responsibility.

To promote community responsibility, Paul Robeson Academy started a program called "Harambee," which many schools have adopted. Harambee (KiSwahili for "we pull together") is how they begin the school day. It includes affirmations, meditations, and visualizations. Harambee is an integral part of the village concept, the system of operation for Paul Robeson. The village concept of schools is that everyone in the village is a teacher, with the parents being primary teachers. At Paul Robeson, the "front door stays open," because the school staff expects the other villagers—local Detroit community people—to come in and participate by bringing their trades and talents, thus fostering a sense of excellence. The philosophy is that everyone is excellent in something; therefore, they are welcome to bring their expertise to the school, thus enhancing the total program operation. Johnson says:

> So we don't have bars for the windows and you don't see graffiti around because essentially we believe in the village concept. This sense of communal school really takes hold and promotes a village-wide sense of pride where everyone has sense of ownership. (Interview, 1993)

In addition to inviting the community to participate in the schooling, the Paul Robeson Academy has made provisions to keep the doors open longer. With coordinated efforts from administrators, faculty, staff, parents, and community leaders, Paul Robeson provides before- and after-school programs, early childhood programs, and Saturday school, and operates on an eleven-month academic school calendar. These programs allow students to participate in on- and off-campus field events, athletics, and cultural and performing arts, as well as study pilot training and accounting and attend other workshops which assist them in their economic, social, and political development.

Among its most recent developments, Paul Robeson Academy has proposed to the Board of Education the boarding-school concept. The boarding-school concept proposes to offer some "transitional" students—those who are placed in foster homes or those who have repeatedly checked into shelters—protection, often from domestic and street violence. This novel component of Paul Robeson will be essential to providing a more stable home than their temporary dwellings to great numbers of abused and homeless youth. This project is expected to be funded entirely by the local community. Johnson explains:

> My role changes at Paul Robeson Academy, not only as instructional leader, but as a community leader. As a community leader, I look for all the resources in the village to impact on these youngsters. Our mission is very clear, and our goals are set in such a way that everyone understands. Paul Robeson is not just a school, but a movement. It has been created to move towards the goal of significance and effectiveness for the entire community. (Interview, 1993)

Emerging African American Immersion Schools

Interviews with Program Coordinator Josephine Hill of Malcolm X African American Immersion Academy and Program Coordinator Anita Sparks of Dr. Martin Luther King Jr. African American Immersion Academy provide an entry into understanding the design and operation of the Milwaukee African American Immersion School concept. In 1991, a study on the progress of American African males in Milwaukee Public Schools (MPS) revealed that more than 80 percent of the 5,716 Black males enrolled at the city's high schools had less than a "C" average, and that 94 percent of the students expelled from the school system were Black males. Milwaukee parents, teachers, and others in the local community agreed that a variety of circumstances led to this discouraging state for Black males, including poverty, drugs, the diminishing Black family, and the lack of positive male role models. But above all else, they all agreed that something had to be done (Whitaker, 1991).

That something became the Milwaukee plan for an all-male school, launched by MPS Principal Kenneth Holt and a citizen's group of Black educators and parents. The committee who wrote the proposal for all-male schools envisioned a school for American

African males headed by Black principals and/or teachers who would be charged with design and implementation of an Africentrist curriculum stressing African and American African history and culture. The program was proposed to assist Black males in building self-esteem and self-confidence, and would promote a love of learning, the essential elements missing from the educative experience of inner-city Black males. The Milwaukee plan called for an elementary school and a middle school with African and American African foci. The school board voted to create two African American immersion schools for Black males. Due to potential lawsuits brought against the Milwaukee Public Schools by the National Organization of Women's Educational and Defense Fund and the American Civil Liberties Union, the Malcolm X African American Immersion Academy, a middle school with nearly six hundred students, and Dr. Martin Luther King Jr. African American Immersion Academy, an elementary school with nearly four hundred students, opened their doors, admitting approximately 50 percent females to their programs (Hill Interview, 1993; Sparks Interview, 1993).

Unique to the Milwaukee School District is an affirmative action policy that prohibited the academies from hiring a predominantly American African staff. Consequently, this prohibition destroyed the possibility of African American immersion academies to employ a predominantly Black male staff, a highly significant component of Africentrist programs.

> Well, our situation, I have to tell you, is very unique. This is an African American immersion program, but we work under a contract that states that we must employ 77 percent European teachers in MPS. Naturally, what would be most desirable is the ability to have majority African American teachers, but this is not the situation. As a matter of fact, when the school was staffed in 1991, we were staffed with 10 percent more African Americans than the contract stated. Well, our teacher's union immediately filed a grievance because we had too many African American teachers in this building. Some eighteen months later, an arbitrator ruled that the superintendent, in fact, had violated the contract, that staffing the school with more than 10 percent African Americans above contract was unconstitutional. Consequently, the union

agreed with the board that they would leave the African American teachers in the building; however, as teachers retired or resigned, they would be replaced with European teachers. (Hill, Interview, 1993)

Both academies are striving for empowerment, but currently operate under a "school coordinating team." Empowerment status would allow the academies autonomy and self-governance and would grant them freedom to regulate critical components of the programs which are under the auspices of the general superintendent's offices.

Parental participation, a major urban problem, is one such critical component of schooling the African American Immersion schools would be able to regulate if they were given empowerment status. Because the academies are not empowered, they can not stipulate what parents must do. At best, through the "Parent Community Involvement Committee," the academies encourage parental involvement and actively seek parental participation. Though Malcolm X and Dr. King Academies have had more active parents "just in the last six weeks than we've had for a while," it would be ideal if the academies could mandate that parents must participate, take a proactive stance in educating their children, and take responsibility for educating themselves (Sparks, Interview, 1993). The academies are creating courses, workshops, and seminars to bring parents into the building to talk about some of the critical issues related to parenting and schooling.

> We want to get parents involved. We have a nice facility here, we have lots of technology here. We have space in the evenings where we want to run GED programs, computer programs, and others, right in this building. Our shop is excellent, excellently equipped with graphics and design capability and all these kinds of things. If parents want, we'd like to bring them in and get them acquainted with what we have in this building and hopefully, help them improve some of their own skills. (Hill, Interview, 1993)

In addition to extensive cooperative training efforts for parents and concern about honing their personal and professional skills, the African American immersion academies are devoted to Africentric teacher and staff development. Many teachers conduct African and American African and multicultural research to assist them in creating lesson plans and instructional materials. Some teachers are still in the beginning stages of grasping Africentric development and seek greater understanding and mastery of how to incorporate African and American African culture and history into their instructional methods and curriculum. However, those who are more proficient in implementing Africentrist curricula assist their colleagues in developing their classes and instructional approaches. During my visit to Milwaukee's Malcolm X, I witnessed the high level of faculty enthusiasm about the incorporation of Africentricity in the curriculum. Two of the language arts faculty hurried to the media center to share with Ms. Hill that as a part of their language arts instruction they would incorporate African and American African culture and heritage in daily vocabulary and spelling exercises. For example, the teacher might say during a spelling test, "continent—Africa is the second largest continent in the world with 11 million, 700 thousand square miles—continent."

All of the faculty utilize various community resources and consult Africentrist literature and techniques to enhance their instructional practices. Among others, the academies subscribe to a variety of African-centered texts, such as *The African American Experience* (from Globe Books), and supplementary history texts such as *African Americans* (from Scholastic) and Jawanza Kunjufu's *Lessons From Black History* (from African American Images).

The academies deem essential to their curriculum an extracurricular component consisting of mentoring and socialization processes development. In an after school rites-of-passage program, community people who are familiar with rites-of-passage programs and experienced in working with young American African males volunteer to mentor American African males. The mentors monitor their academic progress and guide them in career and personal development.

What we're trying to do is to try to improve the skills and self-esteem of all students, improving values for our young people. (Hill, Interview, 1993)

"Getting It Right"

Project Manager Pryce Baldwin Jr. of Helping Hands Project, Raleigh, North Carolina, discovered that even amidst their altruistic purpose of educating American African males they have taken longer "to get off the ground" than other programs designed for Black males (Interview, 1993). In his interview, Baldwin shared the importance of recognizing that even the best-laid plans may require rethinking, revisitation, and reworking before you "get it just right." Further, even when designers of schools and programs for Black males think they have created the perfect model, they should continue thinking and rethinking possibilities for changing Black males in centuries to come.

Helping Hands is a program that experienced a rather coarse beginning, according to Baldwin. Baldwin, a public school district administrator in the Wake County Public Schools, was highly eager to talk about teaching Black males. He said that engaging in dialogue about the issue would force him to rethink his own personal philosophies and discuss the strategies of Helping Hands. Baldwin insisted that teaching Black males is a community responsibility and lamented that only a handful were courageous enough to try to do something:

> It's a real dilemma that we're faced with. And just to see what's going on in the schools. When you walk into office after office after office, what you see predominantly are black males sitting there waiting to see somebody. It's very distressing. And of course, I'm sure you are aware that there fewer and fewer African Americans period going into education, especially males. (Interview, 1993)

The School/Community Helping Hands Project is an effort in grades 3–8 that combines the resources of the school and the community with unique help toward success in school and life. The project was initiated at the insistence of Superintendent Robert Bridges, who had ample experiences as a teacher, an assistant principal, and a principal. Dr. Bridges looked at Wake County Public Schools statistics regarding promotion and retention, drop-out, and others, and he found disparities between Black males and other student populations that did not favor Black males. Dr.

Bridges even went to the prison system and talked to inmates to ascertain from them exactly what got them into that situation.

There were a number of answers that he received, one having to do with something that, I guess, many of us took for granted. And that is that there is someone specifically in your life who sort of pushes you along, nudges you along, and eventually encourages you go in the right direction. (Baldwin, Interview, 1993)

Dr. Bridges discovered another conflicting issue regarding Black males, that is, that there is a "natural" antagonism between males and females. Baldwin explained:

In many cases the Black male inmates came from single-parent families and as they grew older, they began to want to establish that "manly role," and of course, mothers can deal with it up to a certain point, but up to that point, they run into trouble with it, and that was a large part of the problems that got those guys in prison. (Interview, 1993)

In addition, Dr. Bridges initiated discussion about the absence of American African males in the public school. The boys would tend to go to school with the attitude, "Hey, I'm excited about going to school," and pretty soon they looked around and didn't see anyone who looked like them, so they did not relate. To complicate matters, teachers did not relate to Black males. As a result, many students began acting out. Without proper relations of between Black male students and teachers, Black males either became successful in athletics or the arts, or they sought other ways to become important, and one of the ways they did that was through acting out. When Dr. Bridges looked at special classes in the district's schools, Black males were in special programs at a rate disproportionate to the ratio of Black males to others in the system. In fact, special classes were almost totally comprised of Black males (Baldwin, Interview, 1993).

As an educator, Dr. Bridges realized that something was not right, and if we as American Africans assume that all Black males belong in special programs, then that is immensely problematic. In order to determine the strategies which needed to be implemented to counter negative influences affecting Black males, he designed the Helping Hands project, which is basically a mentoring program. The project heavily recruits American African males from the school system, who serve as "personal models" for grades 3–8. In addition, they recruit male volunteers from the community to serve as community models. An objective of the project is address the problems of Black males from two angles, one from the educational arena, the other from the community. Primarily, personal models focused on assisting Black males with problems. These mentors assist Black boys by helping them get organized for school and sometimes helping them complete homework:

> We meet with the kids in the afternoon, after school, and sometimes they do their homework or projects that they have to do, those kinds of things. We also try to develop some leadership skills in them. Now we have a profile for our kids which is one in which we determine that certain kids must have certain qualities in order to be in the program, and this is what the profile looks like, because what we found in the past is that, if we say we have a program that's going to help African American males, right away, teachers, principals, counselors look at the most troublesome kid in that school, and that's an obstacle to overcome to begin with. So what we're looking for are kids who have had some record of achievement, who are not hard core, and who are not special program, and we focus on those. In other words, the child has to have something for us to work with in order for us to work with him, because we're not a be-all, end-all program. We can't solve all problems of the world so, and I think we were very astute in recognizing that there are some other problems out there that someone else has to tackle that we can't deal with as small as we are. (Baldwin, Interview, 1993)

Another problem to tackle in the program is evaluation strategies. Helping Hands began in 1987; the initial group was sixth graders. The project plan was to work with Black males for three years; however, the best-laid plans were considerably altered:

> We worked with sixth graders through their sixth-, seventh-, and eighth-grade years. And after the first year, we recog-

nized right away, we were in the wrong area. It was just a lot of the kids that we had in the program at that time who already had a mindset on what they wanted to do, what they did not want to do, and so we carried that group on through. And I was just looking through our printout the other day, and I think of the hundred and sixty kids we had the first two years, I think we ended up with something like forty-three now who are seniors, which, we don't know what the drop-out rate is or what the moving rate is, but that's a significant loss in terms of keeping up with graduation rates. We decided, in the next three-year cycle, that we would go back to fourth grade. So in 1990, I guess, we started with fourth graders and carried them through fourth, fifth, and sixth grade. What happened in this cycle was, the kids were in elementary school for two years, and then they moved to middle school, and when they moved to middle school, we had a loss, and the reason we had a loss is because we had kids that left. In other words, each of us had ten kids. Two of those kids probably went to one middle school, two went to another middle school, so there was no continuity, and we decided this year that we would start with third grade and focus on elementary schools exclusively as a preventive measure. And our reasoning for that was that we could not follow up with the other kids. So this year we're in third grade. (Baldwin, Interview, 1993)

The excitement of the program continues as the project unfolds and as the true depths of growth and improvements are witnessed. Six years have already yielded significant positive results in the development of these Black males. Active support and participation from the community and other neighboring schools is encouraged to ensure continued success. Through the partnership between schools and communities, Helping Hands has developed the potential to become a viable nationwide model for achievement for advancing Black males.

Projecting Hope

According to founder and director of Project 2000, Dr. Spencer Holland, its primary goal is to provide positive male role models in the

daily school life of inner-city primary-school—aged American African boys. The belief is that by hands-on interaction with positive
adult male role models, especially American African males, in their
daily school activities and at an early stage in the educational process, these boys will be exposed to alternatives to the types of male
role models who often characterize their nonschool environments:

> I began to visit classes and stay for two or three hours, not
> just for half an hour. And lo and behold! things began to dawn
> on me. Good Lord, boys are sitting up here ignoring those
> women! I'd walk behind a boy and say, "Hey, don't you know
> how to do that? The teacher's up there demonstrating." And
> he'd say, "Yeah." And I said, "Let me see it, come on." And he
> would half-heartedly do it. I said, "Come on. No, let me show
> you." And he would do it and the others would follow. I said,
> Hey! OK, OK, singing songs, playing games, the ABC song, all
> of these things that the boys were tagging as being sissies,
> girls do it. Then I began to look at the environments they
> were coming from—single-parent, female-headed households.
> Almost all of these elementary schools are female enclaves,
> particularly primary grade, nothing but female teachers. I
> said, my goodness, these boys are just ignoring women. They
> get tired of it, and this is seen as a female activity and they
> don't come to school with the kinds of behaviors the little girls
> come with to allow them to sit up straight and tall. We have a
> conflict here that is gender based. And that started the fight.
> (Holland, Interview, 1993)

Since many of these boys come from single-parent, female-headed
households, and there are few, if any, adult males on the school
staff, the primary focus of Project 2000 is to have an impact on the
male child. However, there is a strong belief that the presence of
positive adult-male role models has a significant effect upon females in the process as well.

Collaborating with a network of businesses/corporations, col-
leges/universities, churches and community/civic organizations,
Project 2000 recruits adult male volunteers to serve as teacher assistants (TAs) for one-half day per week in classrooms from kindergarten through third-grade:

There are far too many little Black boys that are being left back in kindergarten and first and second grade. This is madness. How can you leave little boys in epidemic proportions back in that area knowing that emotionally and affectively to leave a child back in first grade you just send him the signal that I'm stupid so why should I try? [In a woman's voice] "What do you mean its gender-based just because a boy comes from a single-parent female-headed household? That doesn't mean that family's dysfunctional." Right, right, right. But there's an object missing in that configuration that this boy needs and his mother cannot supply him. What is that? Maleness. How do you function in these environments that you are going to tag female like church and what have you? There are certain behaviors, you can't bring that street behavior in here, you can't bring that male behavior in here particularly in the population of boys that I started with, these, almost all inner city. So I began to visit, and I began to say to myself, I said, listen, maybe if we brought some men into this environment, into the school setting, these boys wouldn't consider this such a female thing. (Holland, Interview, 1993)

Project 2000 was first implemented by Concerned Black Men, Inc., of Washington, D.C., in 1988 at Stanton Elementary School in southeast Washington, D.C., when the class of the year 2000 entered the first grade. Since that time, the program has been established in several communities nationwide. The objectives of the program include:

(1) To instill positive attitudes toward the school setting and increase the academic achievement of primary-grade inner-city boys. (2) To expose inner-city, primary-grade boys to consistent, positive, adult-male role models who serve as teacher assistants to primary-grade teachers. (3) To provide inner-city, primary-grade boys with alternatives to the types of male role models often found in their nonschool environments. (4) To provide inner-city, primary boys with opportunities for one-on-one interaction with adult-male role models in an educational environment. (Holland, Interview, 1993)

From this exposure to male role models, black boys see for the first time, through Project 2000, men in their school environment who are nurturing, loving, and kind. Also, they see men who are there because they want to be there, men who are volunteering, an uncommon sight to these inner-city males who live in environments where often if an individual does something nice, then they are suspect. "What do you want?" We don't want anything from you but you to learn to read, keep your behavior under control (Holland, Interview, 1993).

All Project 2000 programs have some method for evaluating the effectiveness of the intervention. Depending upon the desired outcomes, primarily increased academic achievement of the boys, the evaluation's design and execution can be simple or complex. The Center for Educating African-American Males, in collaboration with the Institute for Urban Research at Morgan State University, has devised an evaluation process which includes survey instruments for collecting data from students, parents, teachers and staff, and teacher assistants, as well as standardized-test scores and end-of-year teacher grades on samples of students in all schools participating in the program. Since Project 2000 was developed to enhance the academic achievement and decrease the discipline problems of inner-city American African primary-grade boys, it is essential that these data be collected and analyzed if substantial change is to be detected and advancements made in the programs made for Black males.

In addition to Project 2000–Baltimore and Project 2000–Washington, D.C., programs have been implemented in Dade County, Miami Public Schools; Paterson New Jersy Public Schools; New Brunswick New Jersey Public Schools; Newark New Jersey Public Schools; Kirkwood, Missouri; Annapolis Maryland Public Schools; and an independent American African elementary school in Chicago. Most of these programs are sponsored by community collaborations; however, Project 2000–New Brunswick is the only fully corporate model where all volunteers are corporate employees who are given release-time from work to participate, and Project 2000–Kirkwood is the only suburban model. Project 2000–Baltimore and Project 2000–Newark are the only two university-sponsored models. All other programs are sponsored by community/civic organizations.

5

Black Male Culture, Power, and Resistance

The belt on his baggy, faded jeans is unfastened and the strings in his $129 high-tech sneakers untied. He's leaning low to one side, arms taking turns trailing behind him as he works a heavy stroll down the corridor. He knows he's as cool as you wanna be. But to the gray-suited, wing-tipped principal up ahead, the profiling Black teenager is sending off a flurry of bad vibes. In fact, he's got all the markings of a troublemaker. His walk alone seems unfriendly enough, but the sexually provocative message of the loose belt makes bad matters worse. And, besides what kind of Black kid can afford hundred-dollar sneakers anyway?

—Richard Majors and Janet Mancini Billson, 1992, p. 8

Historically, American African males, misinterpreted and misunderstood, have nevertheless managed to survive in American public schools. The aforementioned scenario well describes part of the struggle for cultural expression that many Black males undergo in the public school. Solomon (1988) points out that student groups with "distinctive cultures" have simulated associations within school structures, ranging from those who fully integrate into social system to those who vehemently reject it. This has been the case with American African males and their highly "distinctive" culture. In their struggle for survival in the public school, American African males have managed to endure public schooling along a continuum, but basically by two ways. Some Black males "obey school rules, show respect for authority, conform to expectations," and manage to survive the authority structure of the school (Solomon, 1998, p. 1). Other Black males are extremely resistant to school and mainstream authority. The latter, as Solomon analyzed, often represent "lived experiences, systems of practices, and ways of life [different] from those students of the dominant culture." This clash of cultural forms results in conflict. Often, the conflict is demonstrated as Black males

> break school rules, disregard the codes of conduct, strive to impose their own values, beliefs, and dispositions on the dominant school culture. (p. 1)

This relationship of Black males and school authority can best be characterized through the powerlessness, hopelessness, and invisibility of Black males. It is this antagonistic relationship that is a major concern of researchers, school administrators, teachers, parents, and students, and is the impetus for the all-male academy movement. This chapter documents and analyzes the inimical relationship between Black male students and school authority structures in hopes of substantiating the arguments for all-male academies. The paramount inquiry driving this research is the belief of school and community people that the traditional public school can be a vehicle for liberation and achievement for Black males, even though it has historically and systematically failed to educate them. This chapter explores how it can possibly do both.

Why Black Males Resist

Many Black males are required to enroll in public school and participate in a school authority system which deems them invisible, except in negative terms. Black males are not oblivious to the pervasiveness of negative imaging and stereotyping placed on them by society at large and in turn by the public school. Also, they are aware of the minimal expectations that parents, teachers, and society hold for them. Many Black male youth are trapped in powerlessness and hopelessness. Dr. Spencer Holland of the Morgan State University Center for Educating Black Males argues that these pervasive feelings of powerlessness and hopelessness among Black males strengthen the argument for all–Black-male schools. Although Dr. Holland does not view "Black male culture" as monolithic, he does recognize that countless numbers of inner-city Black males are struggling to survive in environments that are immensely "out of control" and inundated by poverty, crime, violence, drugs, unemployment, and homelessness:

> One of the things that we all know intuitively, and I get people to think about, is understanding the powerlessness of being a six-year-old, or a seven-year-old, in an environment that is out of control. For the most part, inner-city America is out of control. I lived in a controlled environment and was still scared. I had a mommy and daddy there. I was never left alone. I never had to worry about food or shelter or clothing, and still there were times I was terrorized in that inner-city ghetto that we grew up in because there was a lot of violence there. So I remember running into bathrooms and hiding. People weren't shooting each other and cutting each other like they do now, but they were hitting each other with boards, and I mean hurting each other. Now that was mild compared to what a six-year-old inner-city Black boy has to live with today. I mean the constant threat of death, having to sleep in his bathtub, not being able to go to the window, early introduction to drug culture. See he's terrorized, and his psychological profile is often very similar to the children in Beirut and all these other war-torn areas of the world. Where can we give him a safe haven? How about the school? And how about bringing some men in there? Men whom they've never seen before, men who often wear ties, and smell good. He'll often say, "Mister you smell so good." I began to recruit and train men and get them to look at the world through the eyes of little black boys. (Holland, Interview, 1993)

Mr. Silas Sloan, social worker and fifth-grade teacher at Kemet Academy, worries that if school systems do not offer redirection efforts for young Black males, they will emulate and reproduce the negative behaviors of models to which they are too often exposed, including many of their parents':

> From drinking, drug abuse, to avoidance of problems, refusal to adjust to school codes, getting on welfare, creating debts, or just having babies, about 70 percent of the time a child will adopt the parent's problem-solving techniques. And these young people ask themselves as they enter that cycle, "Why go to school? Mom's getting big money on the first and the fifteenth of the month, and the welfare pays for gas, food, light, and shelter. Daddy keeps a fat roll of money in his pocket, and he don't even have a job. So why go to school when your basic needs are met? (Interview, 1994)

Seth Kreisberg's (1992) explication of the relationship of power and domination sheds light on the issue of power and powerlessness and resistance for Black males:

> Across a broad spectrum of institutions that shape our lives, people have power over other people; that is, people have the ability to control, manipulate, and coerce other people for their own ends. These relationships of domination are not haphazardly and randomly developed. Rather, the very structures of our society sanction, indeed define and reinforce them. (p. 11)

The ability to control and manipulate others derives from one's privileged access to, and control of, valued resources, such as education, personal wealth, housing, food, and health care. Many Black males are not privy to this control of valued resources, especially education, which Black people have historically felt is the most feasible avenue for American Africans to achieve the status of citizenship. This belief is attested to by Mr. Vernon Stevens, parent of three sons, two who attend Nijia Africentrist School. Because he is recently retired, Mr. Stevens is able to frequently volunteer in the city school district. He recalls a recent visit to an inner-city public school:

> Well, I got an inside look at the public schools and I've had a chance to think about what's going wrong in our schools. It's

amazing to me. I was really taken aback that the public
schools are supposed to be educating our children, but a lot of
times these schools are just bad environments. They're out of
control—totally out of control. Now how students can learn in
some these schools, I don't know. (Interview, 1993)

What Mr. Stevens doesn't know is how Black males can possibly
learn in school environments, which are in fact very similar to
their nonschool environments—antagonistic and not conducive to
learning.

> Most of these schools don't have Black teachers, and definitely
> no Black male teachers or staff, unless he is a custodian, but
> the school has all Black students. Maybe every once in a while
> you see a Black principal or assistant or a Black male coach.
> It's important for Black males to have positive Black male
> role models. These models make them understand that you
> can be intelligent and gives them a little more respect for
> teachers and principals and for their roles. Black males see
> too many young men standing on the corner right at the inter-
> section of the school, hanging around the telephone waiting
> for the phone to ring, doing nothing. (V. Stevens, Interview,
> 1993)

As Mr. Stevens points out, "there is something that has gone awry
in the school system today that is keeping our children from learning." However, the question remains: if indeed the American African male is not "succeeding" in the educative process, how, then, at
the same time, might traditional public schooling be considered a
viable option in assisting him to achieve liberation? Attorney
Marcus Spell, a Kemet Academy parent, is convinced that publicly
funded, Black male schools and programs are at least one possible
solution to this query:

> In any public school, you are going to have children from "bro-
> ken homes," from single-family households and even two-par-
> ent households that are "dysfunctional," just to use that
> catch-all term. But regardless to those very negative influen-
> tial models that many Black males have at home, they need a
> dependable environment where they can lean on responsible

mentors. The mentor would always be there for him and be someone just to be able to tell him that he cares about him. (Interview, 1993)

In his nationwide comparative study of Black cultural forms of schooling, Solomon (1992) addresses this issue. He explains that instead of producing a more literate, employable, and educated group, traditional public schooling for American African youth produces a resistant population. These resistant American Africans often resist in ways that preclude the students' completion of school:

> Within multicultural-racial societies, the lived culture of racial minorities within schools appears to be influenced by their historical and also their emerging relationships with the dominant groups. In the United States, Black Americans' unequal and subordinate structural position and the creative cultural resource they utilize to extricate themselves from this position has extended to Black students' oppositional forms within the schools. . . . Consequently, Black students' cultural forms may be contextualized partly as "students practicing forms of resistance as members of the Black fraction." (p. 249)

In their interviews, several of the participants illustrated the various ways that Black males display "resistance." One example is provided by Ms. Lisa Johnson. Prior to working as head secretary at Kemet Academy, she worked for five years on a clerical staff in the traditional public school. She remembers:

> Black males were some of the most devious acting kids in the entire school system. I mean when it comes to seeing students in the main office to see the principal for discipline problems, when it comes to violation of school rules, suspension, and drop-out, you have to admit, it's the Black male who is always the biggest number. We had some Black males who acted out so bad that they had to participate in partial-release prison programs, and we had some that just would not listen. Not to his parents, teachers, the principals, and sure as heck not to me. (Interview, 1993)

Likewise, during his three-year tenure in the regular public city schools, Charles Spell, a fourth-grade student at Kemet Academy, recalls similar behaviors to those observed by Ms. Johnson. He illustrates how one of his peers "resists" the school homework code:

> Well some of the students liked me, but some of them didn't. Some of them were nice, but some of them didn't like doing what the teacher would tell them. And some of them didn't like reading and spelling or math. My friend Lamar would always make an airplane out of his math homework sheets. And the teacher caught him and got kind of mad. (Interview, 1993)

Dr. Holland maintains that parents, teachers, and others who deal with urban Black males must be sensitized to their inner-city male culture. Additionally, he recognizes that Black males demonstrate an extreme resistance to female teachers within the classroom:

> Well one of the things being ignored is that little black boys are a particular cultural group. When we [educators and researchers] talk about cultural diversity we often don't think in terms of sex, but male and female, even for children, are cultural divisions. When we think of development of instructional practice we should ask: What are the formal and informal settings in which learning takes place? What inhibits or enhances the chances that the learning will stick? What are the conditions that surround the learning environment? For instance, the model, the sex of the model, the race of the model. In other words, we have got to start looking at what is going on in that classroom that is inhibiting Black boys from succeeding, and one of the most salient things that just jumped out at me was they won't copy women. It was so simple it startled me. And I mulled about it and thought about it and wrote about it and it's more and more clear that this is it. (Interview, 1993)

Dr. Holland asserts that Black male resistance to women is demonstrated at a rather constant frequency:

> You sit in a classroom of kindergarten–first-grade boys, they won't do the dancing, they won't do the singing. Now, what is

peculiar about primary years with preliterate people, how do you teach a child that can't read? Well you're always demonstrating and performing. It's performance-based teaching. The teacher demonstrates a skill or a concept and says, "Come on children, show me, come on." And the little boy says, "I ain't doing that." Her gestures, her demonstrations are always feminine. Sometimes she has on all these long fingernails, and rings on every finger, earrings going. So they're up there doing "Simon Says," you know, the records on, and it's got a nice beat, all of this activity and her dress is going, her earrings are still going, she's flapping her hands, and she says, "Come on children, show me. Mario, do you know your right from your left, and your body parts?" You've got to remember, you're talking about people who are essentially ignorant, not stupid, they don't know where their kidney is, or back from front, over from under. We're talking about people who are still having difficulty tying their shoes, getting their mittens on the right hand. We're talking about very basic things that have to be demonstrated. And I simply discovered that the boys wouldn't do it.

The experiences of Dr. Holland's third-grade mentee, Darnell, provides yet another illustration of Black male resistance. Dr. Holland narrates:

Darnell, a third grader, stopped speaking to the teacher. He was a good student and everything, but all of a sudden, he wouldn't talk to her, was mad at her, wouldn't do his work. And I finally got out a piece of him, [in a child's voice] "Well she saw my stuff." I said, "What are you talking about?" [resuming child's voice] "She came into the bathroom, and I was at the thing, and she was running around and she saw my stuff. . . . Made me pee on myself." I said, "Well she didn't mean it Darnell. You know those other boys were in there throwing paper." [child's voice] "I know, I know." When I told the teacher that, this was the woman's attitude toward Darnell, "He ain't got no stuff!" I said, "It's his. And he's six or seven, and maybe he just got introduced to it. "Aw, Dr. Holland." I said, "Oh no, don't 'Aw Dr. Holland' me. Wouldn't want no strange woman seeing my stuff either."

Dr. Holland's plea to help raise women's consciousness in terms of what a little Black boy is thinking and feeling might well apply to anyone who teaches Black males. Furthermore, Black male motives for resistance to authoritative domination must be considered, understood, and reckoned with if Black males are to receive a positive and quality education and succeed in the school environment.

Kreisberg (1992) postulates that domination in schools and society does not function as a "seamless web" (p. 249). Schools not only reproduce domination, but produce resistance to domination as well. Schools are, in fact, sites of ongoing conflict and struggle for control. Kreisberg offers important insights into the possibilities of human agency and educational and social transformation:

> Resistance is readily apparent in most situations of domination. While the mechanisms of hegemony are powerful, they are not all-encompassing, and they are always characterized by contradictions and conflict. The dominated rarely consent fully to their own domination. Many reject the dominator's theories of their inferiority, and they resist the notion that their submission is for their own good. (p. 16)

American African males reject exclusion and marginalization. There is a history and tradition of such resistance dating back as far as the slave era. Genovese (1974) explains, that enslaved Africans developed a culture of resistance to the institution of slavery and demonstrated their opposition through their language and communication patterns, their work rhythms, and their frequent running away from the burden of slavery (qtd in Kreisberg, 1992 p. 17). "These oppositional practices have been lived out and elaborated upon over the years, and constitute core cultural elements in the urban Black community today" (Weis, 1988, p. 185). As demonstrated previously, within the schools, the behavior of Black males parallels those Kreisberg indicated as resistant forces. Many Black males resist doing homework and delay beginnings of classes. They develop intricate systems of deceiving teachers. They smoke cigarettes and marijuana in school bathrooms and sell drugs in school stairwells. They are opinionated with teachers and wear clothes that offend adults. They refuse to participate in some classes and organize to change unfair rules. In fact, there seems to be no imposition of domination that does not simultaneously create forms of resistance. Hegemony is never complete. In the very rejection of domination lies the seeds of transformation and liberation (Kreisberg, 1992, p. 17).

John Ogbu (1988) considers cultural reproduction and resistance in light of class. He explains that cultural reproduction emphasizes the element of resistance or opposition in the dynamic relationship between the culture of the school and that of the student. As formulated by Willis (1977) in his British study and adopted by United States researchers, this illustration of resistance maintains that working-class and minority youth consciously or unconsciously reject the meaning and knowledge taught by the schools and turn to working-class adults or to "street people" as a source of resistance and exclusion (Kreisberg, 1992, p. 17). In essence, they repudiate the schools by forming countercultures which eventually impede their school success and employability in the more desirable sector of mainstream economy. However, they achieve through these cultures acceptance and often a support system deeply rooted in the American African extended-family tradition.

Lois Weis (1988), in her ethnographic study of American African community college students, explains that American African youth do not consciously reject school meanings and knowledge. In fact, she contends, American African youth want to get an education in order to escape from poverty and other problems in their environments. However, no matter how resounding the desire to acquire an education is, American African youth tend to behave in ways that will probably not lead to their school success—for example, excessive tardiness, lack of a serious attitude about school work, and other indications. Unfortunately, this further inhibits their chances of obtaining academic credentials for employment or further schooling in the mainstream economy.

Black Males, Power, And Culture

In the national American African community in general, the concept of Black culture is generally viewed and accepted as a severely limited one (Madhubuti, 1990). For example, the culture of American Africans as a potential force for social, political, and economic development is given very little attention in the education of American African children. Rather, even the education that is received within American African family structures reflects an American European cultural and educative hegemony, which in essence completely whitewashes American African culture. Haki Madhubuti asserts that many American Africans view the concept of "culture" as an invisible entity:

> To most of us, culture, as a concept, is abstract—that is, one does not actually observe culture. Yet, we all experience its manifestations, such as clothing, art, music, housing, weapons, films, literature, language, food, political, educational and social organizations and economic structures. (Madhubuti, 1990, p. 5)

If it is indeed more than mere conjecture that American African culture at large is generally viewed as restricted, then it would be fair to assert that the culture of American African males might be considered an invisible one, unless it is presented, as is most often the case, as a negative entity.

In this regard, Dr. Holland contends, American African male culture might be viewed as a community created by the needs of the people to fulfill and perpetuate themselves, or as an entity that goes virtually unnoticed, or at best is unappreciated (Interview, 1993).

This concept of an invisible and powerless culture most adequately describes the treatment of American African males in the public schools. For example, when inner-city Black males are recognized, they are most often characterized as unlearned, uneducable, hostile, volatile, criminal, and physically and sexually aggressive. They are stigmatized by most Americans as individuals who might take the life of another for a pair of "Air Jordans" or for a Pistons Starter jacket, or who might just take their own lives in the struggle to acquire them. Responses from Holland, Johnson, and Spell bring up the question of whether or not the behaviors of American African males necessarily reflect ill preparation for citizenship or suggest their unwillingness to learn. The paramount concern in our analysis of power and resistance is as follows: Why does the American African male reject school knowledge and meaning?

Dr. Holland's discussion of inner-city Black boys, in light of their massive violent deportment and academic failure, maintains that indeed a Black male inner-city culture exists, and its recognition in negative terms is devastating, especially during the early years of the Black male educative process. It is partially due to this fact that the present educational system is failing Black males (Gourdine and Smitherman, 1992; Holland, 1991; Kunjufu, 1989; Watson and Smitherman, 1992). Researchers have demonstrated that males exhibit different psychosocial and developmental styles; that teachers perceive males differently from females; and that without intervention, these differences can adversely affect the educative process and achievement of males (Soderman and Phillips, 1986). Soderman and Phillips (1986) analyzed a significant body of research on learning and gender differences and concluded that there are at least five areas of difference where young male students are concerned:

1. *Psychosexual differences.* Males, across all observed cultures, exhibit greater aggressiveness, desire to explore, and vigorous rough-and-tumble behavior because of hormones that exist at or before birth. Increasingly, teachers are not willing or able to tolerate these behaviors. Males, in turn, are taking these attributes to extremes and turning them into daring behaviors that cost this society dearly (i.e. vandalism, violence, etc.)

2. *Structural differences in the brain.* Boys appear to experience slower growth in the left hemisphere of the brain. Though the male may perform better than girls on tasks that require mechanical and geometric skill, the delayed growth puts the young male at risk for language and speech problems, stuttering and even allergies. By themselves, these symptoms are not serious, but when combined, they are associated with reading/spelling difficulties, attention and concentration deficiencies, hypersensitivity to criticism, memory, and sequencing problems.

3. *Developmental differences.* In terms of cognitive development, boys lag behind girls anywhere from 6 to 18 months. Their visual development is slower, and boys are physically less mature. Thus a boy who is 6.5 years of age may be

developmentally as young as 4.9 years of age. In school, he may be competing with a girl who is his own age chronologically (6.5), but mentally and physically the girl is 8 years of age.

4. *Academic achievement difference.* Sex differences have been shown to be strongly correlated with academic achievement. For example, when compared with girls, kindergarten boys consistently score lower on tests designed to measure academic potential and language skills.

5. *Differences in perceptions.* Urban males of Color are often feared and perceived as dangerous and in need of control. Biases and expectations have a strong impact on educational and occupational outcomes. Instead of getting the attention, the positive reinforcement, and nurturing that promotes growth and success, males are often labeled slow learners or behavior problems. They are suspended from school, locked up in juvenile detention facilities and adult jails far more often than females and their counterparts from other ethnic backgrounds. (p. 67)

Dr. Na'im Akbar (1991), an American African psychologist, asserts that "maleness" is a mentality that operates with the same principles as biology, that is, it is a determined biological fact which is in no way subject to choice. Dr. Akbar contends that this mentality is dictated by appetite and physical determinants and guided by instincts, urges, desires, and feelings. The male mentality is driven by the immediate relief of tension and urges:

When it is time to use the bathroom, he doesn't say, "Mamma, may I?" He wets on Mamma if she's in the way. When he gets hungry he does not have a concept that somehow says to him, "I am going to eat soon, so I will be patient and wait." His response is, "I want to eat right now!" Neither is he very selective about whether it's done at two in the morning or at noon. (p. 4)

Dr. Akbar maintains the "male mentality" is predicated on a sexist and objectified perception of manhood and predominates only in males who are not willing to take the prerogatives and responsibilities of "real manhood." He contends that in order for Black males to transform into the stage of Black "men" (that is, responsible, productive citizens), their culture and orientation must be understood.

The need to understand the inner-city Black male and to discuss his perception of himself, and the perception of him by others, has been a major research concern of scholars for some years. For example, in *Cool Pose: The Dilemmas of Black Manhood in America*, Dr. Richard Majors (1992), an America African psychologist at the University of Wisconsin—Eau Claire, and Janet Mancini Billson agree that American Europeans often view the lifestyle and culture of inner-city Black males as threatening, aggressive, and intimidating. For much of the past decade, Dr. Majors has studied the culture of Black males and believes the culture of the Black male—that is, his demeanor, speech, gesture, clothing, hairstyle, walk, stance, handshake, and other cultural characteristics—deserves scholarly analysis in order to better understanding his psychosocial development. Majors views the nature of inner-city Black males as "cool pose," that is, he is characterized as "being cool," "with the program," and "in the house." He defines this inner-city Black male disposition as

[a] distinctive coping mechanism that serves to counter, at least in part, the dangers that black males encounter on a daily basis. As a performance, cool pose is designed to render the black male visible and to empower him; it eases the worry and pain of blocked opportunities. . . . Cool pose is constructed from attitudes and actions that become firmly entrenched in the black male's psyche as he adopts a facade to ward off the anxiety of second-class status. It provides a mask that suggests competence, high self-esteem, control, and inner strength. It also hides self-doubt, insecurity, and inner turmoil. (p. 5)

Majors maintains that a major dilemma of the inner-city Black male is his quest to exhibit *masculinity*; he is too often grounded in "masking strategies" that require him to deny and suppress his feelings. He is highly attractive; he is perceived and perceives himself as the epitome of control, strength, and pride. However, even in his "charismatic, suave, debonair, entertaining" persona, he presents himself as a "mysterious challenge" (p. 2). Unfortunately, this challenge is interpreted by society as assertiveness, hostility, and volition. In short, the inner-city Black male is misunderstood. This misunderstanding, Majors contends, can explain the fact that the inner-city Black male dies earlier and faster than American European males from suicide, homicide, accidents, and stress-related illnesses; he is more deeply involved in criminal and delinquent activities; he drops out of school and is suspended more often than American European youth; and he has more volatile relationships with women.

Majors also believes that misunderstanding and misinterpretation of Black male culture by American educators leads to the eventual ruin of Black males in this society. As Majors demonstrates, the "cool posing" of Black males leads to the misinterpretation of Black male expressions by American educators and eventually leads to their educational failure. Majors briefly discusses, but does not highlight, the issue of the misinterpretation of American African males in terms of "black and white."

Summary

In the phenomena of misinterpretation and misunderstanding of the inner-city Black male, unfortunately, much of the incomprehension is expressed by the national American African community. In short, many American Africans have embraced and perpetuated the stigmatization of the inner-city Black male. The concept of being Black and male and inner-city is perceived by many American Africans and American Europeans alike as a negative monolith. The negative image of inner-city Black males is illustrated by the national media on a daily basis. Live coverage of one American African male being apprehended in an undercover police series for beating his girlfriend or yet another being set up to sell crack to an undercover agent is how Americans expect to see American African inner-city males. Also, at noon, six, and eleven, or in any daily paper, Black males are seen in droves, handcuffed or lying bludgeoned on a street corner. And at virtually any hour, a brother might be seen mouthing off on some tabloid television program, boasting his tenure in the local gang or perhaps explaining why "Black men don't pay child support" on the next "Sally." Even on

the "big screen," in an era of the emergence of the most numerous
Black film writers, directors, and producers, *most* American African males are typecast in roles which reinforce complete apathetic
attitudes toward the Black community. Just as the exploitation
films of the late 1960s and the 1970s did, brothers are currently
cast as drug dealers, "gang bangers," gigolos, and womanizers. Unfortunately, these characterizations of Black males display often
undisputed images of Black males as men with low self-esteem and
unrelentless self-hatred. Again and again, in the white media and
in Black films, negative presentations of American African males
prevail.

My greatest concern, however, is that the stereotype that *all*
Black inner-city males are out of control and "out for the kill" has
been abundantly reinforced even by American Africans. These and
any monolithic presentation of a Black male culture is highly disturbing. Black male culture is almost always interpreted to mean
dire trouble and social unrest, and seemingly most Americans are
comfortable with this presentation. Certainly, it makes for fiery
headlines and good copy, but what point is accomplished by continually perpetuating only the fatalistic side of the culture of Black
men?

The shared experiences as teachers, researchers, and most importantly as inner-city American African males by Dr. Holland, Mr.
Spell, and Mr. Stevens highlight major keys to the success in educating Black males. Their position confirms the need for Black
male schools. The personal experiences with inner-city Black males
shared by these Black men themselves confirm that within the inner city exists a part of culture that is truly devastated and
plagued by educational, economic, and political deprivation. In this
culture, corner crack houses, weapons and drugs, teenage mothers,
absentee fathers, and drive-by shootings are a typical, daily reality.
But at the same time, even among this inner-city carnage, many
American African males become great contributors to society and
achieve tremendous feats of success. Many inner-city American African males contribute as law enforcement officials, teachers,
assembly linemen, military personnel, and bankers, as well as su-
perstar athletes and entertainers. Still, great numbers of our inner-city Black males are lost to drug addiction, drop-out, and unemployment. As well, inner-city Black males make up the majority
of the prison population. While few graduate from high schools,

many Black males don't even envision higher education as a possibility. Inner-city American African males represent a high percentage of the entire American African male population, and thus we need to focus on the problems and confront the issues surrounding the demise of this population.

However, one must ask: Where are the "positive" brothers? Do they not exist? Are they not a part of inner-city Black male culture? Before I go further on this issue, I must stop my tirade to say that in my own research, I am guilty of the exact criticism that I am discussing, that is, highlighting the negative statistics and waving the inner-city Black male banner. Why doesn't my own research focus on, for example, the positive attributes to inner-city communities made by fraternities and church leaders, yet another group of inner-city Black men? I emphasize: there is a dire need for us to share "truths," whether ugly or not, and to be brave enough to expose the side of inner-city Black males that is ghastly, but it is also necessary to exhibit the countless brothers in the inner city who are concerned about continual educational development for all children, who encourage citizens to vote, and who take drastic measures to ensure safety in their inner-city communities. These brothers do exist. They are positive and powerful. Is it not the responsibility of the national media, researchers, teachers, and community leaders to highlight the positive side of inner-city Black men as well as present the negative? Not *all* "positive" American African males have joined in the "white flight" to the suburbs in hopes of acquiring a safe haven away from inner-city Blacks. With the constant torrent of negativity toward inner-city Black males, it is no wonder that those who do act out the negative stereotypes, do just that. What other models do they have, other than athletes, a handful of silver screen players, and other entertainers? Is it any wonder that they resist conformity to public schooling and mainstream culture? They do not see enough American African males in other than a negative light.

However, positive American African males do exist in the inner city, but somehow we just do not recognize them. As political, social, and educational leaders, individuals must refrain from telling the world and further convincing inner-city Black males that they are merely an "endangered species," expected to drop out of school, forbidden to apply to college, destined to be unemployed, and somehow to be excused for not accepting responsibility as men. In addressing the question "What are inner-city males made of?" we must present an answer that reflects positive and powerful inner-city Black models as well. We must continue addressing the specific educational, social, and economic needs of the inner-city Black male, and at the same time, teach these young, inner-city brothers that they are developing Black men. Although they are living in a racist, capitalistic, hegemonic society where American Africans have survived by "makin a way out of no way" in many cases, American African males must be convinced that there is a community of concerned American African men and other individuals who will support them in their transition to manhood.

Now, how do we accomplish this task? The answer is that we must demand that our Black males are properly educated. As chapter 6 of this work discusses, we have no choice but to make critical analyses of the public schooling process for American African males. Who is teaching our Black males? How, and through what paradigms, are they teaching them? We start with every man, woman, and child, and we join in a national conversation about what approaches are most appropriate in educating Black males in their particular environments. Then we must insist that teachers teach Black males about achieving liberation and that they treat these Black males equitably.

Appropriately, this chapter ends by returning to the inquiry aroused by the participants: Why do American African males so often reject school knowledge and meaning? Perhaps American African males resist and reject the culture of public schooling because they are aware that it is a myth that schools necessarily adequately prepare them and other students for survival and citizenry in our society. They are indeed aware that schools can assist individuals in personal and social mobility; but at the same time, they see they daily annihilation of Black males in the public schools. Further, it is most often not their fellow American African male counterparts who benefit from public schooling. Perhaps this awareness pushes them toward "countercultures," such as the drug trade and gangs. Unfortunately, these countercultures recognize that these young males are vulnerable and lure them into their families. Every human desires that power be realized. We also desire to be in control of our lives. Public schooling for American African males does not teach them how to obtain and maintain control over and within their lives, nor does it teach them that by simple virtue of being the individuals that they are, they are unique, important, and powerful.

The public schooling research and experiences with American African males provided by the participants of this study confirm for me a need to clear up a longstanding fallacy. That is, we so often look at how much the American African male has failed, that we ourselves fail to look at the nature of how he has been successful. The focus on how little he has done, how lacking he has been, and how far he has to go to catch up with the rest of society has become the backbone for a new pedagogy for teaching Black males. The impact of this phenomenon effects the way in which American Africans learn and must effect the way in which they are taught—in public schools and even by their parents. This pedagogy assumes American African males cannot read on grade level. It dismisses their aesthetic expressions, such as music and dance, as "street culture." Also, this pedagogy diminishes any semblance of agency for American African males. They are most always presented as hopeless victims.

Linda McNeil (1988) supports rethinking the phenomenon of educating groups and individuals based on negative presuppositions. She identifies ritualized patterns of teaching and learning. For American African males, these ritualized patterns have been unequivocally related to their failure in the public school. McNeil says:

> The ways of knowing into which they are initiated helps set students' expectations of themselves as people who can learn, ask questions, contribute new answers, or who must be dependent on others to tell them what they need to know. (p. 207)

There is a need to rethink American African male culture, especially concerning the issues of power and resistance. Instead of dismissing American African males as statistics of drop-out, crime, and violence, more critical analyses might focus on their motivation for acceptance of "countercultures," including the drug trade and others. If indeed their resistance and rejection of public schooling and mainstream culture provides autonomy and a sense of liberation, how can parents and educators who are interested in guiding American African males redirect their resistance to yield "successful" and productive world citizenship and assist them in realizing their power, autonomy, and liberation? Because of the ubiquity of hegemonic, mainstream systems that were not even designed for them from the beginning, it is no easy task. There are no easy answers. However, until paradigms shift in the schooling processes of American African males, they will not be able to direct their extremely powerful selves to the construction, reconstruction, and revision of their own lives and thus rebuild and reclaim their communities and schools.

6

Reclaiming Community, Renaming School: A Community Approach to Teaching Black Males

> If we are seriously interested in education for freedom . . . it is also important to find a way of developing a praxis of educational consequence that opens the spaces necessary for the remaking of a democratic community. For this to happen, there must of course be a new commitment to intelligence, a new fidelity in communication, a new regard for imagination.
>
> —Maxine Greene, 1988, p. 127

Maxine Greene (1988) maintains that in order to achieve a "democratic community," we must consider a "fresh and sometimes startling" pedagogy (p. 127). This new pedagogy would mean providing opportunities to hear the community voices, thus involving the participants who are seldom heard—the community people. This chapter is a proactive stance against the silencing of community people. It hinges, in fact, on Greene's call for "audibility" and the "involvement" of community people in order to create and maintain a "democratic community." From the heard voices and experiences of the school and community people–that is, the students, teachers, secretaries, parents, and administrators, the establishment of

Black male programs demonstrates an attempt by school and community people to "find a way" for "the remaking of a democratic community." If the needs of American African males are ever to be met, public schooling requires major changes. One necessary modification is in the way in which community and schools are viewed, by school and community people alike. Both groups see their domains as separate entities. Changing this attitude has been a major concern and the paramount motivation for the design, proposal, and implementation of alternative schools and programs for American African males. Schools for Black males must be a place where they are prepared for life roles, not merely a place isolated from the mainstream of life where they spend several years concentrating on a curriculum that may not be useful in assisting them in obtaining gainful employment, furthering their education, affirming their culture, and celebrating their heritage.

Schooling, then, for Black males, must be uniquely crafted in order to accommodate their varying learning styles and designed to understand their particular culture. Schools must be community-centered to foster greater neighborhood and citizen participation and oriented to target the specific problems and needs of both Black males and their communities. Anyone who has been tracing the issue of public schooling for American African males might be interested in how these alternative schools and programs are doing in their attempts to promote social change and in their attempts to develop American African males for survival. Who could better address this inquiry than those school and community people directly involved in teaching Black males? This chapter engages us in the schooling, parenting, teaching, administrative, and student experiences of these individuals.

Schooling and Community

The concept of working together as a community is an important component and critical issue in teaching Black males. Though each participant shares in his or her own unique way the individual schooling experiences and associations with alternative schools and programs for American African males, all of their stories and experiences directly connect to the central theme of community. From the stories, it is evident that the community members see a dire need to reclaim their communities and be active participants in the schooling of American African males. The participants illustrate that a greater sense of community, perhaps even a "democratic community," must be achieved as a prerequisite to creating an educative community. A person is a "product" of his or her community or he or she is a counterproduct resulting from resistance to it. Learning to live and work effectively in a community setting is an especially important concern incorporated in the design of Black male schools and programs. Mr. Stevens, a Nijia Africentrist School parent, explains that the philosophy of the school is deeply grounded in the African village concept:

> At Nijia, we are a whole unit, the principal, students, teachers and staff, parents, and the entire local community. Everyone cares about everyone. One hundred percent of the staff cares about child upbringing. We are serious about the village concept, "It takes a whole village to raise a child." In the regular public schools as soon as the bell rings at the end of the day, the teachers and principal and everybody is separated. Basically, when they walked out the door they had no more responsibility. At Nijia, all of the teachers care. I mean all of them. If any one of them can do something for a child there, they will. It doesn't have to be that child's teacher either. Everybody goes out of their way to try to make things run smoothly in the "village." (V. Stevens, Interview, 1993)

Social change is a force which forces community people to form more and more asymmetrical associations, thus weakening ties of locality and community. A goal of Black male schools is to establish egalitarian associations with school and community people. For example, Paul Robeson African-Centered Academy operates on the village concept. This concept is important in the creation of a "democratic community." Regardless of race, class, educational attainment, or other qualities, the unique talents and expertise of all individuals willing to share them are recognized and utilized in this community model. The model provides for students a paradigm for a sense of equality and lessons in respect for humanity.

A student's life affects all facets of his schooling experience. Clearly, school faculty and staff should be able to recognize some of the problems that American African males bring into the classroom from their home environments. Further, when these problems are identified, faculty and staff must show genuine concern and compassion for them and put forth an honest attempt to assist this population. The lack of recognition of these problems by school people was the concern of the several participants. Ms. Fort, Mr. Stevens, and Ms. Johnson are astounded by the treatment of American African males in the public schools. They can not understand why teachers, administrators, secretaries, and others in many public schools are unable to recognize that often times certain behaviors demonstrated by American African males, such as attitude swings, misbehavior, and other illustrations of resistance, can often be attributed to their home environment.

Therefore, prevention, intervention, and remedial strategies must be established by schools and communities for Black males to ensure that parents who are unwilling and/or unable to provide for their children have school and community programs available for them. Further, the participants are irritated by the manner in which public schools handled most behavioral problems as they are identified. That is, the behavioral problems are most often handled in ways that are demeaning, disallowing choices for the student to control his behavior, and denying the students agency.

One participant shares one of her methods for dealing with an American African male in the school upon recognizing his feelings of hopelessness and despair. Ms. Jackie Fort, secretary at Nijia Africentrist School, describes her experiences with Black males from nearly five years of working in the public schools. She indicates that American African males are "ignored," and many do not feel "loved." She deems alternative schools and programs essential to the development of young American African males because many American African males do not get the support that they need from their home environments:

> Well, I know most of the time I saw parents, at Central Elementary, a public school, was when a child was in trouble. You know, a discipline problem. When the school gave programs, the turnout was so low. It would be like three or four parents representing seven, eight hundred students. The administration and staff tried everything to get them to participate. But, it seemed hopeless. The students were very undisciplined and a lot of them, you could tell, had a lot of problems

at home. Unfortunately, we didn't have the staff to really take time with these kids. So a lot of them became castaways that nobody wanted. No other school wanted them, and usually these particular schools, the ones who couldn't handle this population, would get those students. (Fort, Interview, 1993)

Ms. Fort is convinced that a major component in teaching Black males should be to get the parents and community involved in their educative process. Additionally, she recognizes a dire need for school faculty and staff to offer genuine attention and positive affection to Black males in the school system because many of them "do not get this attention at home." She believes that a balance between cuddling Black males and strict discipline should exist, and that discipline may be most effective if it is administered by an American African male:

Our children seem to respect the Black male more; they use that hard voice. They'll listen to our women, but they seem to look up to the men a little faster than they will the women.

Mr. Spell, a Kemet Academy parent, suggests that a lack of participation by parents and community people, especially participation by males, contributes to the inadequate preparation of Black males in the traditional schools:

In terms of trying to get the parents involved—Well, yeah, when Charles was at Hillside, the regular school, they would send notices home, but there was nobody at them, that's the problem. And, there isn't much you can do about that really, except just continue to try. But I think other public schools who have the same problem, after a while, they just give up.

When my wife was teaching, you know, in a poor neighborhood, she would send notices home with the kids and never see the parents. The grandparents might show up, and she had far too many single-parent households. I mean, she had something like thirty-six kids in her class and of that number, this was two years ago, twenty-six of them didn't have a daddy at home. That's a huge percentage. That's unbelievable, so recruitment doesn't help you in an environment like that. You're lucky to get the mamma, and in most cases, she didn't

even get the mamma, she got the grandma. Grandma be raising everybody, mamma and the kids.

What I liked least about Hillside were no men. I mean,
when they had programs which the principal encouraged me
to participate in, I was there by myself. Very few fathers in
the neighborhood participated. (M. Spell, Interview, 1993)

Ms. Lisa Johnson, a secretary at Kemet Academy, expresses
that schools and programs for Black males offer them a "solid, di-
rected academic experience" that they might not otherwise have an
opportunity to experience. She views the academy as an integral
part of the community, and vice versa. Her hope is that this model
of communal love will prove to be the rule, not the exception, for
inner-city communities:

> I remember one particular student who never felt loved
> enough. And one year I made up my mind, I said, I'm going to
> be really nice to this kid. I'm going to really go out of my way,
> I don't mean buying him anything like that, but just showing
> him that he is somebody special, and somebody cares about
> him. The first year, he kept pushing me aside, pushing me
> aside, and he never really trusted me, and I guess he always
> thought there was something underneath all this kindness.
> She's up to something. There must be a reason why she's act-
> ing this way, and then finally, toward the end of the school
> year, just before school let out, he came to me. He sat down,
> and said he just wanted me to know that he was going to miss
> me, and he couldn't wait until school started again. And when
> school opened that next year, he came looking for me. Before
> it was, "Get away from me, get away, get out of here," but he
> actually came looking for me, and it was no more than to say,
> "Hey, Ms. Johnson, how you doing? How was your vacation?"
> This sixth grader had a completely different attitude. And to
> this day, he still comes in every morning, waves, goes to his
> classroom, but it's just to let him know somebody cares. I
> don't sit down and say, "This one I'm going to do this week."
> He was just someone I kept watching, and at first I couldn't
> understand why he was acting the way he was. It was almost
> like he did things on purpose to irritate people. I kept watch-
> ing him, and finally it dawned on me, maybe he just needs a

little more tender loving care. No matter how rushed I was, which I always am, I would stop, speak to him, and always make a little time for him. (Johnson, Interview, 1993)

"Tender loving care" from parents, teachers, administrators, and community people is precisely what Mr. Spell thinks is "missing" from the education of American African males. American African male students need to be provided a guidance system to assist them in their positive development. Since many adult American African males are absent from the household and other caregivers are not capable or able, for various reasons, to provide guidance for their children, this guidance must be provided by all who are involved in teaching them.

For me the key is being there, and sure you have to discipline them, and you have to be tough on them in certain situations, but you have to be versatile, so you got to do both of those things. And when you let them sit on your lap and hug you and rub you on your face and, you know, whatever they feel like doing, then they don't run from you when you get mad. What am I saying? For me, the key to teaching Black males is to try to communicate with them as best I can and try to understand how they feel. Because I think too many men are just stand-offish, and they don't really communicate until their son is in trouble. Sure we can yell at them then, but I mean that's not how you deliver that message. I think that's still got to happen.

And nobody's going to do anything for you simply because you tell them to. If they do the right thing, it's because they wanted to, and if they know that you love them, then that makes them want to.

Well, kids learn by example, so, you know, you got to be the example for them. A lot of examples that they see are athletes. I really don't see anything wrong with that, I mean, you know, there's nothing wrong with aspiring to be a professional athlete as long as you understand that you probably ain't going to get there. Aside from that, I wouldn't discourage them from wanting to be athletes, particularly those who are the best at what they do. Nothing's wrong with them wanting to be somebody that's the best at what they do. So that's why I try to focus on education.

That's what I say, get as much education as possible. I agree, you need the "paper" depending on where you want to compete. You want to compete in the field of education and writing, you have to earn a Ph.D., otherwise you can't play, you know. But if you want to be something else, then maybe you go to a technical school or vocational school. Maybe you go to a school for chefs, but at least that's more education, it's additional training, not necessarily college. The thing is for them to have enough self-worth where they can decide, "I want to be a chef," that's the thing, and if there are too many up there, what do you want to be? You have to find out. Find out that they really like drawing cartoons instead of doing math, he ain't no dummy, he's just got a different talent, and maybe he does not necessarily have to go to college to be a good cartoonist. And that's my philosophy, I'm not going to force my sons to go to college simply for the sake of getting their degree only if its necessary to get where they want to get in life. Because I'm going to help them get wherever they want to go, and if it ain't college, I'm not going to worry, because I have to start off with where they want to go. (M. Spell, Interview, 1993)

Charles, Mr. Spell's fifth-grade son at Kemet Academy, feels that Kemet Academy is helping him "get where he wants to get in life." Charles compares some of his schooling experiences from his former public and private schools to his experiences at Kemet Academy. He comments on the significance of extracurricular programs and Black male models:

Now I'm in the fifth grade. I heard about Kemet about two years ago, when my mom became a staff coordinator. Last year when I was at Hillside Elementary, there was a lot of stuff happening there. I was in there since the third grade, and I was graduating from that school. They had sixth-grade activities, like scavenger hunt. Some of the students were real nice and some of them were on the hall patrols.

I didn't have any male teachers like at Kemet. Studying was not hard for me. I studied every time a test came up. My

favorite day was when we had a party, because I was absent
only twice during the whole year. I didn't have a lot of the
activities, and I didn't have to take a foreign language. I like
school because you get to play games. We have a math game
in division, and you get to write the answer on the board. We
had division problems on the board and whoever got the first
five right could stay up there, and I was the first one up there
because I had more right than my teacher. I could even beat
my teacher.

We didn't have After School and Saturday School at the
other schools. So sometimes on Saturday I would go to a football game. I like Kemet better sometimes because it's in like a
safer vicinity. They have like a different dress code, you have
to wear a uniform.

Taking trips from our Big Brother group is a lot of fun. We
get to go to some colleges and sometimes we stay at Kemet to
talk to them. It makes me feel real good because they teach us
lot of different things. They teach you about the great pyra-
mids, our history and things like that. Yes, I like being at
Kemet. (C. Spell, Interview, 1993)

As each story suggests, developing a greater sense of community
requires that egalitarian relationships among, students, parents,
teachers, administrators, secretaries, and other community people
be strengthened wherever possible.

Summary

Growing up in a small, rural town on the Pamlico Sound in eastern
North Carolina, I recall countless times being lectured to and
sometimes even "given a killing" or punishment by the "elders" in
my community. Seemingly on every corner, a distant uncle or aunt
or just an older person in the neighborhood often caught me in all
my moments of iniquity. Whether I was caught "talking ugly," "acting too grown," or just plain "acting mannish," rest assured some
adult in the community would feel obligated to reprimand me for
my ill behaviors, mention the fact that I came from an outstanding
family, and make no bones about telling my parents about the situation after escorting me home. Even at school, it was the very same

thing. Whenever I was caught waiting to see the principal or standing in the hall with my nose in a circle awaiting my biweekly, sometimes triweekly, paddling, I was certain that by the time I got home, my parents would be well informed of my daily "misbehavins" from an older brother or sister or maybe from my aunt who worked in the cafeteria.

My point here is that there was a definitive institution of neighborhood and community, consisting of parents, teachers, custodians, aunts, uncles, cousins, and others, that I was aware of and feared as a boy and that rarely exists today. Many of the participants on this study shared similar situations reflecting those community ties, and I believe we all wonder what happened to that era when a neighbor could discipline another person's child in good faith and with good intentions, or at least felt comfortable reporting any misbehavior. I suppose the reality is that those days are now obsolete. And though we may decide that we do not wish to return to those days of old, certainly there are some important lessons to be learned from that system of community.

In this chapter, we have discussed that "system of community." We have established that community participation and joint decision-making and establishing a greater sense of community and school involvement provide the most efficient avenue in addressing problems and issues related to Black males. As it is often viewed by school and community people, "community involvement" cannot be limited to dumping off various educational and social problems for solution by local leadership. The need is to educate Black males and all other people for social action. The school people, community citizens, and the public-policy—makers must all work together to help the school become a better institution. The school is one facility that exists in virtually every community, and it is often the only public agency in many American African neighborhoods. Thus, in the education of Black males we must redefine schooling and community and view them as mutual vehicles for strategizing empowered and liberated American African males.

In a truly educative community, all individuals will accept that the education of American African males is a task requiring time and energy on the part of each member of the community. Education then becomes distinguishable from schooling. As "education" is confined to formalized institutions, schooling represents a holistic concept of educa*ting*, the action verb, including the academic, social, and political realms of individuals. Schools operate at the optimal levels from this premise; students, parents, teachers, administrators, and community persons assume new roles, including accepting the responsibility of coordinating all educative, political, and social activities. Education is indeed the sum of many parts, including not only what is available through the school program, but also through the home, the church, the peer group, and the community. Each Black male is reached through some aspect of the community in which he resides. Thus, as indicated in chapter 5, once the ability to "reach him" is realized and his culture and environment are understood, it becomes important for each educator to join in the local discussion of the community.

Becoming a part of a larger educative community will mean some new and even expanded roles for the school. The basic purpose of the school will still be the improvement of the society, the community, and the individual. However, this might mean that in addition to classroom instruction, some teachers will become change agents, some will become ombudsmen, some will work to improve school and community relations, and others will work at developing community leadership.

The school will not forsake transmission of information as an objective, as a community's development is in large part dependent on this style of learning. We need to help Black males learn more *from* the world than just always *about* it. Learning in this sense provides them agency and never compromises the ability to affirm their cultural identity. Further, the educational system could use its knowledge base and professionals' skills on various community improvement tasks involving the schools, the teachers, the students, and the community people. The school could play an important role by helping community residents recognize and carry out various responsibilities. Several of the alternative schools and programs illustrate this *true* sense of community. For example, the Kemet Academy hosts a bi-annual "Sharing and Caring" program. Sharing and Caring is organized and carried out by students, parents, teachers, administrators, and other community people. The program is an effort in which school and community people raise money to provide nonperishable food items and clothing for needy community people. Similarly, at Nijia Africentrist School, the local school and community people, as a part of the socialization process of the students, conduct a community appreciation parade. At this function school and community people witness the need for cooperation and mutual appreciation. Perhaps if all schools and communities would consider these collaborative efforts, then school and community people would be effective agents. They would be better able to reach into every corner of the community, touch every citizen, rejuvenate community pride, and serve as a facilitating agent in helping Black males help themselves.

Even though we may not return to those long-gone community days of yore, as voiced by the school and community people in this chapter, there is a need to reclaim our communities and redefine schooling as a part of them. Each of the participants demonstrates what every citizen needs to do in order to begin our reclamation. They express a commitment to the education of American African males, compassion for and understanding of these males, confidence in the ability for them to learn, and a dedication to their communities and schools.

It has been evidenced through the community of voices articulated in this chapter that a commonality of interest in schooling and community exists in Black male schools and programs. This interest is empowering and enables Black males and individual schools to go from the very bottom of district ranking to the top. Celebrating schooling and community allows students, parents, principals, and teachers to applaud reports of high student attendance, success in passing national and district standardized assessments, and favorable grade-point averages. Most remarkably, the schooling and community models included in this chapter do not require an extensive amount of money, nor do they have unthinkable and unrealistic requirements and time commitments. In fact, anyone interested in educating American African males may very easily emulate the behaviors and adopt the practices demonstrated in this chapter by the school and community people. That is to say, anyone, regardless of gender or ethnic origin, can show sincere compassion and a genuine interest in teaching Black males. Any one can befriend and mentor a Black male. Those who are interested in teaching Black males and believe that Black males can learn, who will be understanding and compassionate, and who will commit to teaching him "by any means necessary," will be the leaders who will exhibit change in the education of American African males in the public schools.

7

Who Will Teach Our Black Males?: "A Call to Action!"

Of the dominant images of teachers, controlling stands out. In almost every form of media, we see the stern, severe looks that have tended to characterize teachers over the decades. Student-teachers are told to "develop a stare," "not to smile until Christmas," or "never to let the class get the upper hand." Control equals classroom management. Being in control shows who's in charge.

—Diane DuBose Brunner, 1994, p. 116

The question "Who will teach our Black males?" has been a major preoccupation of researchers and educators, and, as you will read, is a major concern of participants of this study. This chapter is about models for teaching Black males in the traditional public school and in Black male programs. We are immersed into the world of teachers and teaching and are provided different lenses for understanding how parents, students, and secretaries view teachers and teaching and how teachers see themselves. As Brunner (1994) points out, "control" and "domination" are recurrent themes among teachers (p. 116); this chapter demonstrates these issues.

In the final report to the Committee to Study the Status of The Black Male in the New Orleans Public Schools, Garibaldi et al. (1991) shed insight into the problem of teaching Black males. They report from a teacher survey of randomly selected district teachers two startling findings:

> (1) that almost 9 of every 10 teachers expect their Black male students to succeed; but almost 6 of every 10 believe that their Black male students have positive attitudes about school and value education for its significance to their future. (2) While 16% of the teachers believe that most Black male students they teach will drop out before completing high school, 56%—almost 6 of every 10—do not expect these students to attend college. (Garibaldi, 1991, p. 18)

Although 90 percent of teachers expect their Black male students to succeed, 6 of 10 *do not* think that the males themselves value education and deem it significant. Therefore, the lack of teacher expectation remains consistent.

Because 60 percent of the participants indicated that they were elementary teachers and 16 percent were middle- and high-school teachers, these results will be quite disturbing to those who are concerned about the future of Black males. Garibaldi reminds us that the early grades are the formative years in which high expectations should be encouraged for all students and especially for American African males (p. 18). However, as expressed by my study participants, "poor, negative teacher attitudes" about Black males is a continuing reality. Response from my study participants confirm the aforementioned statistics. In fact, my research participants identified three specific "teacher attitude problems": (1) low expectations for Black males, (2) fear of Black males, and (3) apathy towards Black males.

Mr. Craige Thomas, a fourth-grade teacher at Nijia Africentrist School, suggests that a great part of the schools' failure to provide effective and meaningful educational experiences to inner-city Black males is because of their classroom teachers. In particular, he suggests that the teachers lack leadership and innovation and school systems do not hold them accountable otherwise. His story raises the following questions: (1) What do teachers need to know about the learning styles and teaching environments of their inner-city Black male students? and (2) How will classroom teachers be held accountable for teaching Black males? These questions represent longstanding concerns, as curriculum experts and teachers have been searching for strategies in planning effective teaching and learning methods for American African males. According to Mr. Thomas:

> Inner-city Black males are under harassment from both outside and inside the system. There are teachers who are as burned out as they say the kids are. I used to go into the teachers' lounge, just to sit, you know, hear the "scuttlebutt." You can really hear teachers voice their opinions, and there are some lost brothers and sisters out there teaching our kids who know nothing about the African-centered perspective and nothing about Black culture. So I felt my greatest teaching moments came in the teachers' lounges. These teachers are expecting inner-city Black males to come in, sit up straight, look at them, focus, don't talk, have his pencil, smile, write, read, sit quietly, get up, eat lunch, sit back down. They are all living in a fairy tale. Their expectations were out of line. The teachers were not geared to handle the inner-city Black males.
>
> These kids come home, and momma ain't been home for a week, daddy ain't been home in two days, if he's there at all. So now this kid has to get ready to go to school the next day. I don't know what teacher is about to get him, but I know this kid went through hell last night worrying about his momma. And you [teacher], you want him to do reading, writing, and arithmetic, and this kid has been traumatized? The boyfriend came over, kicked momma's ass up and down one side, and you expect this kid to go and sit down and pay attention. The kid hasn't eaten; his momma, all cracked up, and took the money, all the welfare money, all the food stamp money, and they ain't ate in two good days. Except, maybe, he ate chocolate bars that he'd been stealing from the supermarket. But you expect this kid to come and learn your well-prepared lesson plan, and you want to fault him because you say the kid should be prepared for class?
>
> No, look beyond the classroom. Where does this kid come from? Teachers are not trained in social welfare. They aren't trained to look beyond and see what kind of student they're

getting prepared to teach that day. And that kid may be fine one day. Momma may have done well for the last couple of weeks, but then this is just the week, you know. Daddy promised, ain't seen him but once every other year it seems, and his father promised to take him on a trip that never did materialize. This kid's upset! You can't come near the kid. Oh, I remember one school, a middle school, and a kid came in. The look on his face immediately read, "Bad day, keep the hell away!" I read that on his face. Now if you read this on his face, I ain't about to teach this kid, make this kid sit down and mind me. I just want the kid to sit down and think about whatever is bothering him. And maybe we can talk him through it. "Look, you going to work it out." So I put the kid, kind of big, middle-school kid, you know, about six-two, six-three, good two-thirty, two-forty. There's not too much you going to bluff this kid into doing. So show him you are understanding. I'm sitting there, kid sitting there, doing absolutely nothing but, you know, I told him, "Look, I know you are probably having a bad day. Sit, if you can get the lesson, fine, just try to work this thing out that you're dealing with, and don't disturb the class." That just made his day. No sooner than I get ten minutes in my lesson, here comes this Black female principal coming to *check in*. You know, she's wondering why I'm not sending anybody down to the office. Because I was "freshmeat," they expected about five of my kids to be downstairs in the office for discipline problems that I couldn't handle. She came on in, the kid was doing nothing. He was still sitting there. He wasn't jumping or hollering. She came in, "Mr. Thomas, why is he not participating?" "Ah, excuse me, I sent him over there, he's having a bad day," I said. [Mockingly, in a woman's voice] "He's having a bad day! No he ain't. He don't have no bad day!" "Look, who's in control of this classroom here?" You know, I'm trying to tell her what's going on. I'm giving him an opportunity to think about some things. But she just went off, "You just come down to the office!" And she grabbed the kid. Next thing I know, she has snatched the kid, the kid has snatched back, and we were about to give way to hell. I said to him, "Look, just go ahead, just go, just go wherever she's going, just go with her, don't . . . " "But, Mr. Thomas?" "I know. I know. Just go, just listen to her." That whole scene was unnecessary. That principal had no business doing that, and later I told her, "You don't know what was wrong with that boy. Did you ask that boy what happened in his life? Why he came to school this early? He came to school. Half the battle should be won. He did not become truant. Did you ask him if he was having a bad day?" "No!" They're not trained in social work or social well-being. Teachers don't have that sixth sense of reading a child. They say kids don't read, I say, "There's a lot of reading that you missing too, girlfriend," especially when it come to the Black male. A lot of them have the attitude that "My kid's in private school, so I'm just here to make a paycheck." So they developed an apathetic approach to teaching. And the kids know when you're being apathetic towards them, when you really don't give a shit. Don't give a shit! They can sense it; and with you not giving a shit, they don't give a shit. It was total pandemonium. I talked to teachers, and everywhere I went there might be one or two that were still strong and still had hope and still had empathy towards our Black males. They were being out-screamed, out-talked, lambasted, considered fools and intel-lectually stupid. (Thomas, Interview, 1993)

J. Hare and N. Hare (1991) discuss the need to reevaluate the effectiveness of teachers of American African males in *The Hare Plan: To Overhaul the Public Schools and Educate Every Black Man, Woman and Child.* Because of teacher apathy, fear of Black male students, and low expectations from teachers, Black families have contemplated moving their children out of public schools. Many families have considered private education and even educat-ing their children themselves, in their own homes. Obviously, these considerations do not apply to poor and uneducated American Afri-cans, and Hare and Hare recognize that for most poor children, public school may be the only alternative for being educated. Be-cause of educational hegemony, they do not consider public educa-tion a viable alternative for educating American African children, and as a result, they feel there is no need to save public schools. This hegemony, they argue, effects the entire American African community, but is most often targeted at American African males:

With black boys especially, we are dealing with the products of a broken patriarchy. In a patriarchal racism, it is the male who poses the primary threat to the ruling male, who in his mind can take his place in the bedroom and the board room. Hence a white oppressor must take special pains to suppress the black male. If you kill the male, you do not have to worry about the female and the children, as they are bound to wither away. (p. 9)

This concept is not gender chauvinism, but is rather a biosocial reality and should be understood if public education for American Africans is to be salvaged. Recognition of the misconception of Black male presence as dominating and violent should be calculated in teacher attitudes toward Black males.

Mr. Stevens, a Nijia Africentrist School parent, expressed that dedicated teachers in general, and male teachers and role models in particular, are the most significant factors in destroying these stereotypes of American African males:

At Nijia School, if the students did not learn, the teachers took it personally. Their philosophy is that if a child is not learning, then the teacher may be doing something wrong, and they will do whatever they have to do to make sure that this child learns. In public schools, I did see many students with problems, whether they were learning disabilities or others. I didn't see the support from teachers as far as helping develop that child or helping get that child placed in a program to help him. Now they did have some male mentors in a program in which I participated in, but that only does so much because we only met one day a week.

A lot of the kids are male, but I think that the women often back down from the male kids. If a male kid has a behavior problem, often the female teachers would back away, and then that kid knows that he is in control of that situation. And right then, they've lost him. He asks, "Why should I learn?" I do believe if they had more male teachers that would help. I think that it would offer them a since of identity, because it is difficult for a male child to identify with females. And if you have all female teachers, even the gym teacher was female, then it is really hard to identify with. One of the kids was telling me that he was having problems with some of the other boys. The gym teacher was trying to explain the situation to him. Well, it's kind of hard for a male to go to a female, and say, "Well, I got beat up." She's going to console him, yes. When a father or another male would probably ask him if he tried alternative measures, either discussing it with him, talking to him, or hitting back. Anyway, I do believe that a male presence would help some of the students. Because many of them came from homes that were all females. Many of them run over their mothers, so they figure they can run over the female teachers too. (V. Stevens, Interview, 1993)

Dr. Holland agrees and suggests that societal fear of Black men and boys, even little Black boys, has been transmitted to the classroom. Holland explicates interaction strategies with female teachers:

We take Black men into the public school classrooms and show them the very basic things they will be asked to do in the classroom as models for Black boys, anything that's going on, cutting up paper, handing out paper, marking homework while the teacher's busy putting the grades in her book, anything she needs. We ask the teachers to sit down and draw up a list of tasks and activities they want the men to do. And at the top of the list, their number one choice, was help us with the discipline of the boys. We're talking about first graders, and here you got grown women saying, "I can't handle these little boys." And I say to them all the time, "You're thirty-two and he's six. This is on you. This is not on him. He's not going to rape you!" There's not a six-year-old boy in this world that I would let intimidate me. But this is a lot of what's happening, the adultification of boys. Black boys, just sitting in the corners. Go in inner-city classrooms, you'll find almost a boy in every corner, first isolation away from the group, "Get away from us. I don't give a damn what you do over there, as long as you don't bother us." So he doesn't learn. (Holland, Interview, 1993)

Hare and Hare also purport that the attitudes that many teachers have toward teaching in public schools, especially when teaching American African youth, need to be examined. Apparently, many of these teachers do not want to be in that environment:

Teachers themselves, when they desire to move up, tend to
consider moving out of impoverished schools a virtual neces-
sity—the farther out the better. In any case, when once they
have demonstrated a modicum of innovation and superiority
in the classroom, they typically are transferred out of the
slums to teach middle class children (often white). (p. 5)

This system of teacher promotion is a highly popular trend. Conversely, the researchers lament that demoted teachers, along with
teachers up for early retirement, are often sent back to schools
with poor, American African populations. In fact, the "good" American African teachers are the most solicited to teach in the suburbs
or at "alternative" white schools in the city.

Mr. Spell, a Kemet Academy parent, observes that two major
problems exist with public school teachers which prevent them
from adequately educating American African males: (1) teacher attitudes toward American African males are unacceptable and (2)
teacher attitudes towards their own profession reflect a sense of
professional insecurity. Mr. Spell sees a dire need for American African male role models to teach, and he urges school districts to
recognize an appreciation for public school:

Before my sons went to Kemet, they were in regular public
schools. I mean, they had programs which the principal encouraged me to participate. That's why it's important to have
Black male teachers. It's important for a couple of reasons.
Number one, the positive male role models make children understand that you can be intelligent and it gives them a little
more respect for the role of teacher and the job itself. And
then, number two, they see too many young men standing on
the corner, hanging around the telephone waiting for the
phone to ring, doing nothing. And they need to see successful
Black businessmen doing their jobs. They don't even think
about that. They don't have any idea what it takes to be successful in the business arena, because you can't take them to
the office with you. But if they had more Black male educators right there in their faces everyday, then that provides
them with a different view of what a Black man is supposed
to be able to do. And that's the biggest reason why we should
have more Black male teachers, but until they start paying

teachers what they are worth, their won't be any. There's no Black male influence in the public schools. At least there's not enough Black male influence, and the person that is there is saddled with disciplinary problems for the entire school instead of being allowed to teach. There are too many teachers in the public school system not teaching. They go to work everyday, and they basically are jail keepers. They spend their entire day running down kids, disciplining kids, howling at kids, shouting at kids, trying to keep kids in line, and when the kid walks out of there at the end of the day, they ain't taught him a damn thing. (M. Spell, Interview, 1993)

Mr. Stevens agrees and expressed total disgust with the public schools from his son's experiences in the traditional public school:

I put my son in Nijia because I was already involved in a male outreach program associated with the school. I got a chance to meet some of the teachers. And from that standpoint, and I don't know if this is a crack or what on the public school system, however, his third grade teacher was white and basically she had the attitude that these kids are innercity district kids, if they learn they learn, if they don't they don't. I don't really care. Every PTA meeting she would leave early. They're scheduled from 3:30 to 5:30, and she leaves at 4:00. You go in there and you ask to see the homework, the homework is not graded. He's not even getting a grade for the homework. So basically she's starting to give homework to pacify the parent because you're complaining about homework. So, I think right then that's what really got me. You have teachers who are in the district school system who are not held accountable for the kids who are not learning. There are some problems kids true enough, and I know they have a large class, but if they could save one kid or teach one child, then fine. Well, from her standpoint, she wasn't even going to do that much. You know, I just want to collect my paycheck and go on about my business. If I meet a bright kid then, fine, your son, he is smart, well-mannered. That's how I was brought up, and that's how my son is being brought up. She knew that she didn't have to worry about him, so basically that was just one less kid that she didn't have to care about or pacify or pacify the parents. That's when we made the switch to Nijia School. (V. Stevens, Interview, 1993)

Mr. Stevens also offered suggestions for teacher improvement:

Holding the teachers accountable would have made my experience, my family's experience, at these schools better. I think that the teachers, my son's teachers, did not have a study plan or a study guide for the kids. If we're going out of town, and he misses a day, and I ask what his homework is so he won't miss it because he won't be here next week, she didn't even know that. So basically, she went day to day and didn't even have a schedule of activities for the classroom. I think a teacher should have, I thought that most teachers use, a curriculum guide or a syllabus. She didn't even have that. And, the homework was so shabby. And I know that some of these schools are really hurting for funds. But giving a child homework that's unreadable, you don't know if a number is a 2 or a 5. You don't know which to multiply by. I think the public schools probably get dumped, and since it's predominantly Black, you have to wonder what happens to all the tax money that goes into the schools. Why can't they afford equipment to print legible homework and legible reading material for these kids? If you can't even read it, how do you expect the child to learn?

In *Empowering African-American Males To Succeed: A Ten-Step Approach For Parents and Teachers,* Mychal Wynn (1992) agrees that teachers must reexamine their approaches to teaching American African males. He asserts that the support system for American African males in the public schools must be strengthened. He maintains that teachers and parents represent the paramount variable which provides a foundation for learning for American African males to achieve academic, economic, and social excellence:

We must raise our expectations of our young men to greater levels of achievement in all . . . areas. . . . We must consistently communicate our expectations of excellence; that we not only believe that they are capable, but we expect them to excel. We must establish and reinforce their personal responsibilities, character, and behavior in a manner consistent with our expectations of exceptional goal achievement. We must begin to look at, speak to, and encourage our young men in a way that communicates that we believe that they are capable of owning businesses and rebuilding their communities; that we expect them to take responsibility for, and ownership of, their lives and their communities. (p. 61)

Wynn asserts that teachers must be aware that Black males represent a "complete spectrum of American life" (p. 7). He reminds teachers that Black males come from different communities, family backgrounds, economic statuses, and social strata, as well as single-parent and two-parent households, even within their inner-city culture.

Our classrooms, schools, homes, and communities should consciously affirm that our young men are capable of not only striving for excellence but of achieving excellence. . . . When a young [Black] man sets a goal, . . . we must communicate in everything that we say and do: "You have the power to do that!" (p. 61)

Other researchers agree that the classroom is the place and that teachers are the individuals to affirm for Black males that they have the ability to succeed. However, high expectations for Black males and support for their academic, political, economic, and social success do not exist to much extent among teachers in traditional public schools.

Ms. Josephine Hill, program coordinator and media specialist of the Milwaukee Malcolm X Academy African American Immersion School, describes the struggle to prepare teachers to educate American African males by educating them about American African culture and history:

In June of 1991, the staff [that] was presently here was given an opportunity to transfer, and the people who wanted to be a part of this program were given an opportunity to stay. At that time, two-thirds of the staff left, so there was only a third of that old staff who decided to stay, and other people from across from the district chose to transfer in. One stipulation for becoming a part of this school is that all teachers were required at the end of three years to have acquired eighteen hours of courses dealing with the African American experience. Those courses could include the learning styles of African Americans, the impact of racism on African Americans in this country, courses dealing with African American history, courses dealing with African American culture. The initial group of teachers that came in 1991 knew what those expectations were, so we're working toward that end. We've had three university courses dealing with the African American experience offered right here in this school in the last two years. We're trying to prepare teachers in that way. (Hill, Interview, 1993)

Additionally, Ms. Hill asserts that merely gaining knowledge of African and American African culture and history is insufficient. She asserts that to truly prepare teachers to educate American African males, teachers must "commit themselves" and actively participate in the culture and environments of American Africans:

I think that teachers have to be people who are going to focuse on what is happening in the African American community. I think teachers have to be an active part of that community, people who seek out all these additional resources that you might even listen to African American radio stations, read the African American community newspapers, a person who just really wants to work in this building, I think that they should immerse themselves in the African American culture, history, the entire experience. They need to go out into the community, attend community meetings, maybe even visit an African American church, It's just that a course is not going to do it. Reading a book is not going to do it. When teaching African American males, or any kid, I don't care who that kid is, you have to be able to pull from your own personal experience.

Summary

Unfortunately, many of the 2.5 million teachers that educate our youth in the public schools, male or female, American African, American European, or otherwise, hide behind their desks and witness countless Black males fall through the cracks during the schooling process. Other teachers actively make provisions to remove Black males from their classes and out of their sight through special-education placement and suspensions. Unfortunately, many of these same teachers will continue to teach Black males.

Ideally, the optimal learning environment for teaching the Black male is to provide him with a competent and dedicated American African male teacher. Certainly, this is not to suggest that women and non–American Africans are unable to teach Black males. In fact, Black women and others have educated Black males for years. However, positive American African male role models, especially Black male teachers, are rarely available for Black males. In all of the alternative schools and programs designed to educate American African males, and in a few innovative public and private schools, Black men are recruited to serve as mentors and role models and are trained to instruct them in their classrooms.

Black male organizations, fraternities, lodges, and social clubs as well as sororities, churches, and civic organizations must reevaluate their commitment to the national American African community. Any American African male who does not place high on his agenda the intention to organize a mentoring program, tutorial, "Rites of Passage" program, or other auxiliary to teach or guide American African male youth should understand that he is not a part of the solution. This is a challenge for all American Africans, American African organizations, and non–American Africans alike to initiate programs and demand that Black males are better educated by using their personal, group, and community resources, financial or otherwise, to sponsor Black males.

"Who will teach our Black males?" Every community will teach Black males. Every man and woman who will commit themselves to uplifting their ambition and who will be sensitive and understanding of their culture and environment, and who will demand the highest academic performance—they will teach Black males. As well, those who will employ variant teaching styles and methods and affirm their individual and cultural worth—they will teach them. And finally, those individuals who will model for them the quest for liberation, and most importantly, teach them that they will never be "truly" liberated until all humankind over the world is liberated—they will teach Black males.

8

Conclusion: Ain't Done with My Journey— Teaching for the Promise

Through this work, I have attempted to illuminate some critical questions involved in teaching Black males. The preeminent inquiries guiding this research were as follows: Why have traditional educational systems been unable to teach a great number of American African males? Do alternative schools and programs for American African males better educate American African males? What factors account for alienation of American African males in our traditional school system? What role do curriculum and instruction, parental and community involvement, self-esteem, and ethnic pride play in achieving successful, effective alternative schools and programs for American African males?

This work does not contain all of the answers, nor does it provide a complete, succinct, and error-free paradigm for teaching Black males. This study should be regarded as an illumination of an educational phenomenon and remains incomplete until American African male students are provided optimal learning opportunities in the public school. This work should not be regarded as a "how to teach Black males" schemata. Rather, through the testimonials of the students, parents, teachers, administrators, and secretaries of alternative schools and programs, this work is a progress report of the impact these schools and programs have made on American African male students.

A major frustration throughout this research has been that instead of providing sound, specific answers for many of the questions guiding this research, I found upon investigating one inquiry that such probing usually lead to illumination of another. At any rate, this work should prove useful for anyone who teaches American African males, who wishes to design and implement a school or program for American African males, or who is interested in conducting research which investigates American African males and their plight in America.

This work has proven for me to be extremely gratifying. This is namely because it is a work which provides a platform for "the people" to speak about an educational, sociological, and political issue, as not merely a research interest but rather a personal crisis effecting their livelihood, their quality of life, their very existence. The goal of this study was to present the voices of students, parents, teachers, secretaries, principals, and directors of alternative schools and programs for American African males. Through their shared stories of their experiences with Black males, I sought to provide analysis of the plethora of issues and concerns involved in teaching Black males. I have discovered that three basic components were consistent in the design and implementation of alternative schools and programs for Black males. They were (1) early intervention with infusion of American African male models, (2) gender separation, and (3) incorporation of Africentricity in the curriculum. From the experts in the field, those parents, students, teachers, principals, and directors of alternative schools and programs who are involved with large populations of American African males, I found that a host of strategies, methods, and male development processes were employed to ensure their academic success and cultural survival. Among these strategies were single gender classes, recruitment of American African male models, infusion of African and American African culture and history within the curriculum, class rotations, teacher rotations, mandatory parental volunteer programs, rites-of-passage programs, extended academic year and extended day programs, and others (see appendix A).

Most significantly, from the thirty interviews with administrators, secretaries, students, parents, and teachers, three major themes were most recurrent in the data analysis. The three issues were (1) the need to understand Black male, inner-city culture (chapter 5's focus); (2) the need to encourage unification among school and community people (chapter 6's focus); and (3) the need to reevaluate teachers for Black males and monitor teacher attitudes toward them (chapter 7's focus). These issues are a major concern of the participants in this study and need to be a paramount focus of anyone involved in educating Black males, especially those who wish to design and implement alternative schools and programs.

Implications for Future Research

This study is believed to be the first comprehensive examination of alternative schools and programs designed to educate American African males. Essential to its objective was to highlight and encourage further research into the schooling process and socialization of American African males. From this research, at least four areas of research in alternative schools and programs for American African males merit further academic examination: (1) school and program history, design, and implementation; (2) development of Africentric curriculum and materials; (3) sociological analysis of Black male culture; and (4) teacher training and development and teaching styles.

First, to understand the effectiveness and impact that alternative education schools and programs have had on Black males, it is necessary to conduct long-term examinations of the historical emergence of the Black male programs. It is helpful to examine the following questions: Who designed the school? What philosophy, mission, and rationale were envisioned for the school? What program features exist in the school? How is the philosophy and mission of the school and program changing? How is the curriculum changing? Additionally, it is necessary to analyze those who oppose the schools and programs and to understand the rationale for their opposing views.

Further, there is a dire need for examination of curriculum materials used in alternative schools for American African males. In the national American African community, the tradition of survival and "makin a way outta no way" is highly prevalent. Many Black male schools and programs have managed to "squeeze blood from a turnip," and they have been able to employ an Africentrist curricu-

lum by effectively pulling together African- and American African–
centered instructional materials to use for their appropriate grade
levels. Many of the schools and programs supplement the district
curriculum with recommended African and American African and
multicultural materials. However, there is a great need, in all disciplines and on all grade levels, for development of Africentrist
textbooks, teaching manuals, student guides, and curriculum
models. These curriculum materials may offer consistency in the
Africentrist curriculum. As well, these materials will assist in providing sound, scholarly guidance to understanding world concepts
and different peoples of the world.

Other investigations should continue to examine the culture of
Black males. There is a great need for comprehensive analyses of
Black males in the public schools, in the inner city, in rural Amer-
ica, at the university, and in the prison system, just for starters.
Further studies are needed that discuss what it means to be Black
and male in America. Panoramic and realistic presentations of the
Black male experiences are needed to assist those who are inter-
ested in educating Black males.

Because the teacher is indeed the catalyst in the educative process, it is he or she who has the power to educate or miseducate,
profess or detest, empower or disenfranchise. There must be a
reexamination of teacher attitudes toward American African
males, as well as a reconfiguration of the teaching styles most suit-
able for Black males. Teachers of American African males must be
committed to this population, show compassion and understanding, and be confident that these students can learn.

Prospecting Inquiries

Another question illuminated through this research journey relates
to the ultimate purpose of education for American African males.
In the interviews, virtually every participant in this study alluded
to the fact that the purpose for educating American African males
is to prepare them for world citizenship and to teach them to become positive and productive community members. None of the
data support allegations regarding alternative schools and programs for American African males made by the National Organization for Women or the American Civil Liberties Union that these

schools and programs are elitist, racist, separatist, and sexist. To the contrary, the all-male academy movement is illustrative of the national American African community recognizing problems within its own community and making reparations to do something about the problem. As fourth-grade teacher Mr. Silas Sloan of Kemet Academy reminds us:

> Teaching Black males is not an educational phenomenon, but what is a phenomenon is why public schools have failed to teach them. (Sloan, Interview, 1993)

Indeed, the problem is not in and of itself American African males. Rather, the problem is the fact that the public education system into which they are thrust does not appropriately educate them.

The hour is here; it is imperative that parents, students, community leaders, educators, and researchers who are interested in teaching Black males take control and make a promise to the countless numbers of American African males who are continually miseducated in the public schools. The national American African community and others interested in teaching Black males should continue research and teaching in hopes of finding the most optimal conditions in which American African males may be educated. We should, then, design, implement, and maintain community schools and programs that will teach Black males.

APPENDIX A

Black Male School and Program Features

SCHOOLS	SG	AA MALE MODELS	AC CURR.	CR	TR	MAN. PAR. VOL.	RITES OF PASS.
Malcolm X—Detroit		*	*			*	*
Malcolm X—Milwaukee		*	*				*
Martin L. King—Milwaukee		*	*				*
Paul Robeson—Detroit		*	*			*	*
Programs							
C.E.A.A.M.—Baltimore	*	*			*		*
Helping Hands—Raleigh	*	*			*		
Morehouse Mentoring—Atlanta		*					*

SG—Single Gender; AA MALE MODELS—American African Male Models; AC CURR.—African-Centered Curriculum; CR—Class Rotations; TR—Teacher Rotation; MAN. PAR. VOL.—Mandatory Parental Volunteer; RITES OF PASS.—Rites of Passage

Black Male School and Program Features (*cont.*)

SCHOOLS	LANG.	UNIF.	PS	MS	AS	SS	EAY	MHV
Malcolm X—Detroit	*(2)	*	*	*	*	*	*	
Malcolm X—Milwaukee		*	*	*	*			*
Martin L. King—Milwaukee		*	*	*	*			*
Paul Robeson—Detroit	*(4)	*	*	*	*	*	*	
Robert Henson—Baltimore		*						
Programs								
C.E.A.A.M.—Baltimore		*				*		
Helping Hands—Raleigh		*						
Morehouse Mentoring—Atlanta		*						
My Brother's Keeper—E. Lansing		*				*		
Raamus Academy—Cincinnati		*				*		

LANG.—Foreign Languages; UNIF.—Uniforms; PS—PreSchool; MS—Morning School; AS—After School; SS—Saturday School; EAY—Extended Academic Year; MHV—Mandatory Home Visit

APPENDIX B

Addresses and Contact Numbers for Alternative Schools and Programs for American African Males

Malcolm X African-Centered Academy
Principal: Dr. Clifford Watson
6230 Plainview
Detroit, MI 48228
(313) 271-8637

Marcus Garvey African-Centered Academy
Principal: Harvey Hambrick
11131 Kercheval
Detroit, MI 48214
(313) 245-3267

Paul Robeson African-Centered Academy
Principal: Ray Johnson
13477 Eureka Street
Detroit, MI 48212
(313) 368-6982

Dr. Martin Luther King Jr.
African American Immersion Academy
Principal: Josephine Mosely
3275 North 3rd Street
Milwaukee, WI 53212
(414) 562-4174

Malcolm X African American Immersion Academy
Principal: Kenneth Holt
2760 North 1st Street
Milwaukee, WI 53212
(414) 264-0160

Ujamaa Institute–Medgar Evers College
Director: Basir Mchawi
New York Board of Education
Brooklyn, NY 07189
(718) 935-3904

Coldstream Elementary School
Principal: Nora Williams
1400 Exeter Hall Avenue
Baltimore, MD 21218
(410) 396-6443

Robert Coleman Elementary School
Principal: Attie Johnson
2400 Windsor Avenue
Baltimore, MD 21216
(410) 396-0764

George G. Kelson Elementary School
Principal: Angie McCullum
701 Gold Street
Baltimore, MD 21217
(410) 396-0800

Matthew A. Henson Elementary School
Principal: Leah Hasty
1600 North Payson Street
Baltimore, MD 21217
(410) 396-0776

Pine Villa Elementary Schools At Risk Male Class
Principal: Willie J. Wright
North Grade Elementary School
Dade County Public Schools
Miami, FL 33055
(305) 624-3608

Stanton Elementary School
Principal: Elbele Davis
Alabama Avenue and Maylor Road SE
Washington, DC 20020
(202) 767-7053

East End Neighborhood/East
East End Neighborhood House
Dr. Paul Hill
Cleveland, OH 44104
(216) 791-9378

Cleveland Public Schools
East Cleveland Public Schools
Attn: Connie Calloway
Cleveland, OH 44104
(216) 268-6596

Fulton Academics and Athletic Magnet/San Diego City Schools
San Diego City Schools 92114
Principal: Carol Pike
(619) 262-0777

The HAWK Project/Grant Union High School
Sacramento, CA 95838

The Institute for the Advanced Study of Black Family, Life and Culture
Executive Director: Wade Nobles
Oakland, CA
(415) 836-3245

Grant Union High School
Principal: Richard Owens
Sacramento, CA 95838
(916) 921-3757

Helping Hands Project
Project Manager: Pryce Baldwin Jr.
Wake County Public Schools
3600 Wake Forest Road
P.O. Box 28041
Raleigh, NC 27611
(919) 850-1660

Inroads/Wisconsin Inc.
Director: Debra A. Kenner
231 West Wisconsin Avenue, Suite 903
Milwaukee, WI 53203
(414) 272-1680

"Man To Man"/Paul Robeson Academy
Founder: Ray Johnson
13477 Eureka Street
Detroit, MI 48212
(313) 368-6982

Manhood Incorporated/Marcus Garvey Academy
Principal: Harvey Hambrick
11131 Kercheval
Detroit, MI 48214
(313) 245-3267

"My Brother's Keeper" Program/Malcolm X Academy
Michigan State University
Co-Founder and Director: Dr. Geneva Smitherman
Co-Founder and Principal: Dr. Clifford Watson
221 Morrill Hall
East Lansing, MI 48824-1036
(517) 353-9252/336-3608
(313) 271-8637

Project 2000
Center for Educating African American Males
Morgan State University
Director: Dr. Spencer Holland
Baltimore, MD 21239
(410) 319-3275

"Save A Star" Male Leadership Development
Monnier Elementary School
Principal: Omelia T. Shaw
13600 Ward Street
Detroit, MI 48227
(313) 270-0071

Woodward Elementary School "Stars" Mentoring Program
Principal: Judith Jackson

2900 Wreford
Detroit, MI 48208
(313) 494-2501

Black Male College Explorers Programs–A&M College
Tommy Mitchell
Tallahassee, FL 32307
(904) 599-3483

Children of the Sun/Tampa Urban League
Garry Mendez Jr.

National TRUST for the Development of African American Men
908 Pennsylvania Avenue, SE
Washington, DC
(202) 543-2407

The Greater Tampa Urban League
TRUST Director, Wally Shabazz
Tampa, FL 33605
(813) 229-8117

Concerned Black Men, Inc.
President: Broderick D. Johnson
1300 Seventeenth Street NW, Suite 1
Washington, DC 20001

Morehouse Mentoring Program
Morehouse College
Atlanta, GA 30314
(404) 681-2800

PROJECT ALPHA
James Bland III
Alpha Phi Alpha Fraternity, Inc.
National Headquarters
2313 St. Paul
Baltimore, MD 21218
(410) 554-0040

Responsible African American Men United in Spirit
(RAAMUS Academy)
University of Cincinnati

Cincinnati, OH 45221
Founder and Director Dr. Kenneth Ghee
(513) 556-5553

Toussaint Institute Fund, Inc.
Director: Gail Foster
1851 Adam Clayton Powell Jr. Blvd., Suite 20
New York, NY 10026
(718) 875-5469

APPENDIX C

Pryce Baldwin Jr., Project Manager
Helping Hands Project
Wake County Schools
Raleigh, NC
October, 1993

I really believe that there has to be gender separation for a time to help each Black male learn what it is to be a Black man in America. We have three special schools in our county. We have a school that we call "Re-Direction," which is for middle-school kids who've gotten off the track, and they go there and stay for stay for the remainder of their middle-school years. Then we have "Longview," which is a school for the really troubled kids, and these are for high-school kids; and then we have "Phillips School," which is an alternative school, and this is for kids who choose, who decide, "I don't want to go to school anymore, but here's an alternative for me." The times are varied such that kids can work and go to school. A lot of the girls have children, they have a nursery there where they can go, that kind of thing, but I have always believed, and I will believe it until I am proved wrong. I think that kids that really have difficulty in a traditional school need a setting that is away from the maddening crowds. They can go to school for four hours, they can take other kinds of training in vocational areas, they can grow their own crops, they can build their own buildings, they can do whatever they need to do, and I think that's the answer. I mean, building prisons is not the answer, because once a kid goes in, when he comes out, even in the training schools where they send kids who have criminal profiles early on. I mean that's a waste of resources, and I've looked at some of the boot camps that they have around the country

123

where they have kids who have gotten into trouble, and they go there and they come out, and I think that's a part of that whole idea.

Ray Johnson, Principal
Paul Robeson African-Centered Academy
Detroit, MI
December 1993

Paul Robeson Academy averages about three hundred people who come through the school per week to volunteer and offer services. It drives the staff crazy since the building is rarely ever closed. They can hardly find the time to get things cleaned up. In the last year or so, I guess we had over eleven hundred visitors from around the world that come in unexpectedly. A lot of that has to do with, initially, I think, the novelty of the male academy, but what has kept it going has been the way we do schooling in a manner that is not traditional. We attempt to create a environment that positively child-centered, where there's going to be a lot of love, a lot of security. School climate becomes very important, and the climate we want to send is one of not only friendliness, but one of warmth and one that indicated that in this place you are special, you are loved, and we're gonna take care of you. And so we try to feed the emotional needs as well, through reinforcement of the positive self-esteem, through their own history and cultural identity, through validating what they have in their homes, and by connecting with their families, so the climate says, it is warm, it is outgoing, we love you, you will be safe here.

Josephine Hill, Program Coordinator
Malcolm X African American Immersion Academy
Milwaukee, WS October 1993

I transferred to this school because of the program, it's number one. I wanted to be a part of a program that worked and dealt with trying to improve the condition of African Americans. This school is 99 point 9 percent African American, we are in a very economically, I'd say, deprived area of the city. This is an attendance area school, so this is just a situation here that maybe, it's a concern to the city because maybe we don't have the parents at this point who work with their kids as conscientiously as some people do and for various reasons, maybe they're working a full-time job and maybe they're single so that job, you know, kind of takes away from the time that they could spend working with their child. Maybe they have some kind of sickness or illness, or just whatever the reasons are, we need to focus over here on getting more parents involved in the school situation, consequently getting more involved with their child, but I can say what has happened here since the focus of the school changed with the addition of the new program, the community has come forward and taken a very concerted look at this program, a very interested, hard look at this program. The community wants this program to be successful. We've had community people to come in and say, "What can I do, I want to be a part of this program, I'm very supportive of this program." We have people from across the city who are inquiring about this program who'd like to bring their children in here. We have a higher quality or caliber of student who lived in this attendance area who transferred out, who's starting to transfer back in, and this is the initial year, I mean last year was our very first year, but because of the name change and getting the word out that the focus of this program is changing, we're getting some very positive press. People are hearing, and we're trying to promote positive things that we do in this building. We're all just working hard to make a difference. Our students perform much higher than those tests indicate. So we have a, you know, good group of students here, and we're trying in all ways that we can to make a difference.

Dr. Spencer Holland, Director
Project 2000
Center for Education African American Males
Morgan State University
Baltimore, MD
October 1993

Being an educator and a trainer of teachers, you're always dealing with pedagogy. How do you get this information? What are the instructional strategies? What do you have to know about children in order to get them to do what you want them to do?

Now, if he doesn't do it, if Mario doesn't learn the ABC song, which is a major step in learning his ABCs, he's not going to learn to read. I would ask first graders, "All you people, how many in here are having problems reading?" And they are very honest at that level. They raise their hands. I said to the ones that were having problems, "Now, all of you stand up. Do you know your ABC song?" Well, almost all are boys. "Let's sing it." And you could see they hadn't memorized the song. So one of the techniques I used was, let me show you how to sing this song, silently. It's called thinking, and nobody can know. You can do it while you're playing basketball, or you can do it while you're walking in the street. I know why you won't sing it, but I also know that if you don't sing this, you're not getting out of first grade. That's your first smack. Then you're going to have problems with primary grades, and phonics and all of that. So, I'm going to help teach you, make sure you know how to sing this song. Simple. He sings it with me. "Come on, come on. "A-B-C-D- . . .' Come on say it again, Willie, '. . . E-F-G- . . .' Charles, lets do it again. '. . . Q-R-S- . . . " You've got to do this over and over and over and over and over. He does it for me.

Anita Sparks, Program Coordinator
Martin Luther King African American Immersion Academy
Milwaukee, WS
November 1993

We have a new program and it's going well. There are some logistical set-backs, for example, we don't have all of our uniforms for the students yet. But we are determined to do everything we need to do to provide the quality educational experience for our students that we know they deserve. The teachers, staff, everybody is excited about working in this program, and by putting our heads together and working on the same goals for our students, we will get them accomplished.

Dr. Clifford Watson, Principal
Malcolm X African-Centered Academy
Detroit, MI
November 1993

There are some schools and programs that say they operate with an African-centered focus. In order for an African-centered program to work they must understand the entire concept of Afrocentricity. Essentially, when we talk about African-centered education, we take it from the stance that African is the center of civilization. So at Malcolm X, our children are the center of education and grounded in an African-centered philosophy. We educate them from the standpoint of knowing their history and developing a sense of humanity for all people. From this perspective, they are trained to have a clear self-perception of who they are, where they came from, and they know that everybody is part of one big human family that originated in Africa.

Interview Excerpts From Phase Two Study Participants

Charles Spell, Fourth Grade
Kemet Academy
December 1994

I study like every time a test came up. I like to read and do math sometimes. My math teacher plays a math game everyday, "masters of division," to see who can get the right answer to the math problem. And I get it
right all the time. I even beat the teacher.

> Attorney Marcus Spell, Parent
> Kemet Academy
> December 1994

Well before Kemet Academy, they just started that two years ago, I had no
formal teaching experience. I had just worked with Youth Forums speaking to youth groups and to elementary school youth. I went back to school
for a Master's in Educational Leadership, but I decided that this was
something I want to pursue as a career. Education is my calling. So the all-
male school was introduced, and I began teaching.

> Lisa Johnson, Secretary
> Kemet Academy
> December 1994

It's certainly hectic for one thing at Kemet. Well, you have a lot of parents
coming at you, phones ringing constantly, PA system going, and students
coming in. And that's a normal day. That's normal. I'm responsible for a lot
of different things. The biggest thing are the deadlines. You have a lot of
deadlines in the schools, and in trying to meet your deadlines, with everything else, students and everything else, that's kind of hard to do.

> Silas Sloan, Fourth-Grade Teacher
> Kemet Academy
> December 1994

I think that we have really been approaching the whole issue of schooling
Black males wrong. We defend this educational task by pulling data that
Black males are "endangered species" or we look at the this, that, and the
other negative features of Black males. Teaching Black males is not a phenomenon. It's what we should be doing anyway. The phenomenon can easily be put into this question, Why have we failed to teach Black males?
That's the phenomenon.

Rodney Stevens, Fifth Grade
Nijia Africentrist School
December 1994

When I was in the fifth grade, there was a split class, fifth and sixth, and my brother was in my class. Well, he kept me out of trouble. Well, my big brother doesn't have to wear a uniform cause he goes to Whitehills Middle School, and they don't have to.

Vernon Stevens, Parent
Nijia Africentrist School
December 1994

At Hillside, in the regular school most of the black males were non-teachers. Even his gym teacher was a female. You know he had, matter of fact, he only had one male teacher, and he was his kindergarten teacher. Most of the teachers there were female. I wanted him to go to a school where he would have positive Black males around him like here.

Jackie Fort, Secretary
Nijia Africentrist School
December 1994

Most of the time that you really saw parents at the other public schools was when a child was in trouble, the disciplinary problems. That was pretty much the only time you actually saw some of the parents. When they had programs, the turnout was so low, it would be like three to four parents out of seven, eight hundred students. The students were very un-disciplined and a lot of them you could tell they had a lot of problems at home, but unfortunately we didn't have the staff to really take time with these kids and so a lot of them were throwaways that nobody else wanted. No other schools wanted them, and usually these particular schools would get those students.

Craige Thomas, Fifth-Grade Teacher
Nijia Africentrist School
December 1994

The ideal Africentrist school would be a program set up so that the first thing I would do is hire dedicated teachers. I would make sure that they understood where we were as far as mission and curricula. I would test them for curriculum knowledge, but also in value orientation. What are your values? Are you your brother's keeper? Do you understand this concept? that concept? Write a letter to me explaining it.

APPENDIX D

Parent-Teacher Interviewing Instrument

How do you incorporate parents/guardians as a part of their child's learning experience? Do you have specific parental components established? Do you require participation? How important is parental involvement to your institution? to you?

Community Involvement/Collaboration Efforts:

What programs, opportunities, exposure do you offer to redirect American African males outside of school? What strategies do you use to best ensure that students are productive, community-oriented citizens? Do you have outreach programs that teach children concepts of responsibility and commitment to their community?

Teaching Styles:

How do you prepare teachers who are willing to teach at an American African male school, but who may not feel equipped to educate American African males? How do you feel about the presence of American African male role models? Other role models? Do you consider early intervention strategies? Do you recruit American African male role models? How? Why? Have you been successful in your recruitment? Are these American African male teachers teacher-certified? Is certification problematic?

Male Responsibility/Socialization Process:

Do you incorporate a Rites of Passage component? How? Why? What programs do you implement? (e.g. 10 points, KWAANZA)

Uniqueness:

Describe how your school/experience is any different from a traditional school in your district? Do you employ Saturday school? After-school program?

Other:

How do you deal with the issue of coeducational opportunities? Is Special Education an issue? Do you track students at your school? On what basis?

Are your American African male students performing better in this school? How do you know? How do you measure effectiveness of your program? What criteria are used? What results can you share?

APPENDIX E

School Interviewing Instrument

Student Interview I

What school did you attend before Kemet Academy?
What was the school like?
How did you get along with other students? teachers? principal?
What kinds of classes were offered? What were your grades like?
Describe what you liked most/least about your school?
When were you absent from school?
What activities did you participate in at your school? Describe the types of activities that you liked most/least?
Can you describe a day at your school that you really felt important, really special?
What do you miss about being at your old school?
In what ways did your caregiver participate in school activities with you?
Describe the types of teachers that you had. Can you describe your favorite teacher? Why was she/he your favorite teacher? What did you like about him/her? Did you have any Black male teachers?
Were you involved in after-school and Saturday school programs? If yes, which ones? What did you do in these programs?
If not, what did you do after school and on Saturdays?

Parent Interview I

What school(s) did your son attend before Kemet Academy?
What was the school environment like there?

133

How did he get along with other students? teachers? principal?

What kind of curriculum did the school use? Did he make good grades?

Describe what you liked most/least about his school?

Was your son absent from school very often? Why?

Did the school offer activities for your son after school and on Saturdays?

What are your feelings about your son receiving ample attention needed to survive in the school? Explain what ways the school could have provided better services for you and your son.

In what ways were you active in the old school?

Were any of the teachers Black males? Do you think that having Black male teachers is important to your son's education? Explain.

Were there other Black role models at the school? In what capacity? Do you think that these models are important models for your son?

What do you miss most/least about your son's school?

Do you think that your son had good self-esteem as a student at the old school? Why? Why not?

Teacher Interview I

Where did you teach prior to Kemet Academy?

Please describe the school, the curriculum, teaching responsibilities and noninstructional duties, staff composition, etc.

Describe what experiences as a teacher with young Black males confirm or disconfirm the various claims of Black males as an "endangered species."

What type of parental and community involvement was required or solicited at your school? Do you agree with the school policy?

Secretary Interview I

Where did you work prior to Kemet Academy? Describe the school and work environment.

What were your job responsibilities?

Were parents very active in the school? In what ways?

What were the students like at your school? Describe the most memorable student, teacher, parent.

Do you think from your interactions with Black males that your experiences confirm or disconfirm the notion of Black males as "endangered species"?

Do you believe that the young Black males had positive self-esteem?

How could your school have been improved to make the learning experience better for young Black males?

Student Interview II

What grade are you in? When did you first hear about Kemet Academy? What did you think about coming to Kemet Academy at first?
When did you come to Kemet Academy? Why did you come?
Describe how you felt the day you found out that you were accepted to Kemet Academy? Do you remember your first day of school at Kemet Academy? Can you describe what that day was like?
Do you think that Kemet Academy is different from Whitehills School? How is it different? What kinds of classes are offered? Do you participate in after school and Saturday school? What do you do? Do you make good grades? What are your favorite classes? Why?
Can you tell me a bit about what an African-centered school is, like this one that you attend? Can you describe the Rites of Passage program that your are involved in? What do you think about going to school with girls? Do you think it would be better to go to school with boys only? Why? Why not?
Do you like wearing a uniform?
Do you attend school often at Kemet?

Parent Interview II

When and how did you find out about Kemet Academy? Describe the application procedure. When were your notified that you son would be attending? How did you feel about his acceptance? How long has your son been at Kemet Academy? Is the school different from Whitehills School? In what ways are the schools different? In what ways are they similar? Are you pleased with the differences? Why?
What are your feelings about an African-centered curriculum? What does it mean? Do you think that your son understands this concept? How does this curriculum affect your son? you? the community?
What is Rites of Passage? What is your position on the Rites of Passage for young Black males? What do you think about coeducational opportunities? Do girls and boys study better in schools apart or together? Why do you think so? What does your son think about this issue?
Do you feel that your son is receiving a better education at Kemet Acad-

emy than at Whitehills? How do you know? What results can you share with me?

Has Kemet Academy affected your son's level of self-esteem?

Teacher Interview II

Who decides which texts are to be used in your classroom?

Do you develop any material yourself/ How do you incorporate African and American African culture and history? How do you define *African-centered?* Do you believe that the concept is understood by students? parents? teachers? administrators? staff?

How are parents involved in instruction at your school? in your class? What is your position on recruiting Black males in Kemet Academy? other role models? How can teachers be prepared to teach at an African-centered academy who do not have experience with American African and African culture and history? What is your association with Rites of Passage? What is your position on coeducational opportunities? Do boys and girls study better in separate classrooms? Why? What experiences have you observed that confirm your opinion?

Secretary Interview II

Why did you apply to work at Kemet Academy? Why were you selected to serve as an employee? What is your role at Kemet Academy? How important is that role to the functioning of the school? If you could and wanted to, how would you change your role in the school? What is the mission of Kemet Academy in your opinion? Is that mission being met? How do you know? What results can you share regarding teachers, students, etc. that suggest that Kemet Academy is indeed showing results? What do you like most/least about Kemet Academy?

Interview III

Interview III explores the meaning the participant makes of her or his experiences shared in the precious interviews. I will ask the participant to reflect on what she or he has said about experiences before and since becoming associated with the alternative education school or program, and I will ask how she or he understands this experience (What patterns will repeat?) The objective of interview three is to record how the participant makes sense of details reported in the previous interviews.

BIBLIOGRAPHY

The Abell Report. Jan/Feb 1991. Vol. 4, no. 1. Published as a community service by The Abell Foundation, Baltimore, Md.

Agar, M. (1992). Toward an ethnographic language. *American Anthropological Association 84*: 779–795.

Akbar, N. (1982). *From Miseducation to "Education."* Jersey City, N.J.: New Mind Productions.

———. (1991). *Visons for Black men.* Nashville: Winston-Derek.

Asante, Molefi Kete. (1988). *Afrocentricity.* Trenton, N.J.: Africa World Press.

———. (1990). Kemet, Afrocentricity and knowledge. Trenton, N.J.: Africa World Press.

Asante, Molefi Kete, and Abdulai S. Vandi, eds. (1980). *Contemporary Black thought: Alternative analyses in social and behavioral science.* Beverly Hills: Sage.

Ascher, Carol. (1991, June) School programs for African-American males . . . and females. *Phi Delta Kappan* 4:1–3.

A school for Black males; Is it an answer for Baltimore. The Abell Report.

Bell, Derrick. (1987). *And we are not saved: The elusive quest for racial justice.* New York: Basic Books.

———. (1992). *Faces at the bottom of the well: The permanence of racism.* New York: Basic Books.

Brown, Jessamy. (1991, 12 June). Coleman School's all-male class a success." *The Baltimore Sun.*

Brunner, Diane D. (1994). *Inquiry and reflection: Framing narrative practice in education.* Albany, NY: State University of New York Press.

College Entrance Examination Board. (1985). *Equality and excellence: The educational status of Black Americans.* New York: CEEB.

Comer James P., and Alvin F. Poussaint. Raising Black children: Two leading psychiatrists confront the educational, social and emotional problems facing black children. New York: Plume.

Department of Health and Human Services. (1985). Report of the Secretary's task force on Black and minority health. Vol 1. Washington, D.C.: DHHS.

Detroit Public Schools. (1993). Establishing the normative culture. Detroit: DPS.

Eubanks, Dayna. (August 16, 1996). Black male academies. *The Dayna Eubanks Show*. CBS–WJBK.

Fletcher, Michael. (1992, 4 Feb.). Project 2000 needs a few good men. *The Baltimore Sun*.

Freeman, Gregory. (1992, 2 Oct.). Volunteers man school project. *St. Louis Post-Dispatch*.

Frey, Daniel R. (1992). Miracle or mirage? Social science and educational reform for African-American males. Senior thesis. Princeton University.

Garibaldi, Antoine M. (1988). Educating Black male youth: A moral and civic imperative: An introspective look at Black male students in the New Orleans public schools. New Orleans: Orleans Board, 1988. ERIC ED 303 546.

Gates, Henry Louis Jr. (Winter, 1993–1994). Quoted in Does Academic Correctness Repress Separatist of Afrocentrist Scholarship? In *The Journal of Blacks in Higher Education*, no. 4: 40–45. New York: CH II Publishers, Inc.

Gibbs, Jewelle Taylor. (1988). *Young, Black, and male in America: An endangered species*. Auburn, NY: Auburn House.

Giroux, Henry A. (1988). *Schooling and the struggle for public life*. Minneapolis: University of Minnesota Press.

Ghee, Kenneth L. (1991). The RAAMUS Academy handbook for improving academic achievement and cultural awareness in young African Americans (ages 8–15).

Gourdine, Angeletta, and Geneva Smitherman. (1992). "By any means necessary": An interview with Dr. Clifford Watson, On the Malcolm X Academy and the Black all-male school movement. *Toward the curriculum of struggle*. Trenton, N.J.: African World Press.

Gourdine, Angeletta, Geneva Smitherman, and Clifford Watson. (1992, 31 Aug.) Strategies for educating African American males: The Detroit model: First annual report of the Malcolm X Academy, an African-centered school. Detroit: Detroit Public Schools.

Greene, Maxine (1988). *The dialectic of freedom*. New York: Teachers College Press.

Grover, Herbert J. (1991, Jan.). Private school choice is wrong. *Educational Leadership*, p. 63

Hayes, Arthur. S., and Jonathan M. Moses. (Fall, 1991) Detroit abandons plan for all-male schools, citing bias. *Equity and Excellence 25*, 1: 40–46.

Hare, Nathan, and Julia Hare. (1991). *The Hare plan: To overhaul the public schools and educate every black man, woman and child.* San Francisco: The Black Think Tank.

Hill, Paul, Jr. (1992). *Coming of age: African American male rites-of-passage.* Chicago: African American Images.

Holland, Spencer H. (1993). *Project 2000, Operations Manual.* Baltimore, Md.: Morgan State University, Center for Educating African-American Males.

———. (1992). Same gender classes in Baltimore: How to avoid problems faced in Detroit/Milwaukee. *Equity and Excellence 25:* 40–46.

———. (1991). Elementary and secondary education–special populations: Positive role models for primary-grade Black inner-city males. *Equity and Excellence 25*, 1: 40–46.

———. (1989). Fighting the epidemic of failure: A radical strategy for educating inner-city boys. *Viewpoint 28:* 25–28.

Hughes, Langston. (1965). Harlem. *Selected Poems.* New York: Knopf.

Irvine, Jacqueline Jordan. (1990). *Black students and school policies, practices, and prescriptions.* New York: Greenwood Press.

Kreisberg, Seth. (1992). *Transforming power: Domination, empowerment, and education.* Albany, N.Y.: State University of New York Press.

Kunjufu, Jawanza. (1991a). *Black economics: Solutions for economic and community empowerment.* Chicago: African American Images.

———. (1991b, 10 Oct). The real issue about the male academy. *Black Issues in Higher Education,* 63–64.

———. (1989). Children Are the Reward of Life. Chicago: African American Images.

———. (1987). *Lessons from history: A celebration in Blackness.* Jr.–Sr. High Edition. Chicago: African American Images.

Leake, B. L., and D. O. Leake. (1992). Islands of hope: Milwaukee's African American Immersion Schools. *Journal of Negro Education 61:* 1–24.

Lubeck, Sally. (1988). Nested Contexts. In *Class, Race, and Gender in American Education,* ed. Lois Weis. Albany, N.Y.: State University of New York Press.

Madhubuti, Haki R. (1990). Black men: Obsolete, single, dangerous? In *The Afrikan American family in transition: Essays in discovery, solution, and hope.* Chicago: Third World Press.

Majors, Richard, and Janet Mancini Billson. (1992). *Cool pose: The dilemmas of black manhood in America.* New York: Simon and Schuster.

McNeil, Linda M. (1988). *Contradictions of control: School structure and school knowledge*. New York: Routledge.

Luttwak, Edward N. (Winter, 1993–1994). Quoted in Does Academic Correctness Repress Separatist or Afrocentrist Scholarship? In *The Journal of Blacks in Higher Education*, no. 2: 40–45. New York: CH II Publishers, Inc.

Moss, Bill. (1992). *School desegregation: Enough is enough*. Columbus, Ohio: Danmo.

My Brother's Keeper Program. (1991). Unpublished brochure. East Lansing: Michigan State University.

National Center for Disease Control. (1983).

National Coalition of Advocates for Students. (1986). *Barriers to excellence: Our children at risk*. Boston: NCAS.

Perkins, Eugene. (1991). *Home is a dirty street: The social oppression of Black children*. Chicago: Third World Press.

Peterkin, Robert S. (Dec. 1990–Jan. 1991). What's happening in Milwaukee? *Educational Leadership*, 67–69.

Office of Community Service. (1993) Morehouse Mentoring Program brochure. Atlanta, Ga.: Morehouse College.

Ogbu, John U. (1988). Class stratification, racial stratification, and schooling. In *Class, Race, and Gender in American Education*, ed. Lois Weis. Albany, N.Y.: State University of New York Press.

Project 2000 Trainer's Manual. (1991). Published by the Center for Educating African-American Males. Baltimore, Md.: Morgan State University.

RAAMUS Academy Handbook. (1991). Published by RAAMUS (Responsible African American Men United in Spirit) Academy. Cincinnati, Ohio: University of Cincinnati.

Ravitch, Diane (Winter 1993–1994). Quoted in Does Academic Correctness Repress Separatist or Afrocentrist Scholarship? In *The Journal of Blacks in Higher Education*, no. 2: 40–45. New York: CH II Publishers, Inc.

Taylor, Lottie I., and Joan R. Pinard. (1988). Success against the odds: Effective education of inner-city youth in a New York City public high school. *Journal of Negro Education* 57: 347–361.

Sadker, David, and Myra Sadker. (1994). *Failing at fairness: How America's schools cheat girls*. New York: Scribner.

Seidman, I. E. (1991). *Interviewing as qualitative research: A guide for researchers in education and the social sciences*. New York: Teachers College Press.

Smitherman, G., ed. (1980). *Black English and the education of Black children and youth: Proceedings from the National Invitational Sym-*

posium on the King *Decision*. Detroit: Wayne State University Press.

Soderman, Anne K., and Marian Phillips. (1986). The early education of males: Where are we failing them? *Educational Leadership*.

Solomon, R. Patrick. (1988) Black cultural forms in schools: A cross national comparison. In *Class, Race, and Gender in American Education*, ed. Lois Weis. Albany, N.Y.: State University of New York Press.

Success quiets controversy: Detroit's African-centered academies for boys. (1994). *Black Issues in Higher Education, 10*, 26: 64–66.

The State of Black America. (1992). New York: Urban League.

——. (1993). New York: Urban League.

——. (1994). New York: Urban League.

Tobin, Karen. (1994, 6 April). Afrocentricity in the Public School. St. Louis Post-Dispatch.

U.S. Census Bureau. (1981).

Vega, Marta Moreno, and Cheryl Y. Greene. (1993). Voices from the battlefront: Achieving cultural equity. Trenton, N.J.: Africa World Press.

Wake County Public School System. (1993). School/Community Helping Hands Project. Brochure: Project model. Raleigh, N.C., Wake County Public Schools.

Watson, Clifford, and Geneva Smitherman. (1992). Educational equity and Detroit's male academy. *Equity and Excellence 25*, 2: 40–46.

Weis, Louis. (1988). *Class, Race, and Gender in American Education*. Albany, N.Y.: State University of New York Press.

West, Cornel. (Winter 1993–1994). Quoted in News and Views: Cornel West Moves North in *The Journal of Blacks in Higher Education*, no. 2: 9. New York: CH II Publishers, Inc.

Whitaker, Charles. (1991, March). Do Black males need special schools? Educational experiences with boys only classes arouse hope and controversy. *Ebony*, 54–57.

Wiley, Ed, III. (1993, 11 March). Too few higher education initiatives aim to reverse plight of young Black males, say education experts. *Black Issues in Higher Education* 10: 18.

Willie, Charles V., ed. (1994). *The education of African-Americans*. Cambridge, Mass.: William Trotter Institute, University of Massachusetts.

Woodson, Carter G. (1933). *The mis-education of the Negro*. Reprint. Trenton, N.J.: Africa World Press, 1990.

Wynn, Mychal. (1992). *Empowering African-American males to succeed: A ten-step approach for parents and teachers*. S. Pasadena, CA: Sun.

INDEX

Abell Report, 9

Africalogy, 24

African Americans, 55

African American Experience, The, 55

Africentricity
  defined, 22, 23, 24
  in the public schools, 20–25

Akbar, Na'im, 75

Alpha Phi Alpha Fraternity, Inc., 39

alternative schools and programs, 29–40, 41–62
  Community-Based Male Programs, 38–40
  Evolving Male Schools, 31–32
  School Affiliated Male Programs, 34–38
  Single Gender Classes, 32–34
  Whole Male Schools, 31

American Civil Liberties Union, 12, 13, 14, 19, 26, 31, 49, 53, 112

Asante, Molefi, 22, 23, 24, 44

Ascher, Carol, 29, 30, 32, 33, 34, 37, 38

Baldwin, Pryce Jr., 41, 57, 58, 59

Billson, Janet Mancini, 63, 76

Black Male College Explorers Program—A&M College, Tallahassee, 38

Bridges, Robert, 56, 57

Brunner, Diane DuBose, 95

Center for Educating African American Males, 36

Children of the Sun/Tampa Urban League, Tampa, 38

Clark, Kenneth, 8

Coldstream Elementary School, Baltimore, 33

College Entrance Examination Board, 3

Concerned Black Men, Inc., Washington, D.C., 38, 39

Cool Pose: The Dilemmas of Black Manhood in America, 76

Cremin, Lawrence, 4

Cruse, Harold, 24

Dayna Eubanks Show, 13, 14, 15, 19

Detroit Malcolm X African-Centered Academy, xi, 13

Detroit Male Academy, ix

Detroit Public Schools, ix, x, 13, 31

East End Neighborhood House, Cleveland, 34

Empowering African-American Males To Succeed: A Ten-Step Approach For Parents and Teachers, 104

Failing At Fairness: How America's Schools Cheat Girls, 16
Franklin, John Hope, 8
Frey, Daniel, 9, 10, 15, 16
Fulton Academics and Athletic Magnet, San Diego, 34

Gates, Henry Louis Jr., 20, 21
Garibaldi, Antoine, 96
Gender Issues, 12–20
Gibbs, Jewelle Taylor, 1, 12
Giroux, Henry, 2
George G. Kelson Elementary School, Baltimore, 33
Gourdine, A.K.M., 11, 74
Greene, Maxine, 24, 83
Griger, Keith, 10

Hare Plan: To Overhaul the Public Schools and Educate Every Black Man, Woman and Child, The, 99
Hare, Julia, 99, 101
Hare, Nathan, 99, 101
The HAWK Project, Sacramento, 34, 35
Helping Hands Project, Raleigh, 34, 35
Hill, Josephine, 52, 54, 55, 105, 106
Holland, Spencer, 10, 11, 12, 41, 59, 60, 61, 62, 65, 69, 70, 71, 73, 74, 78, 101
Holt, Kenneth, 52

Illich, Ivan, 4
Inroads/Wisconsin Inc., Milwaukee, 34, 35
Irvine, Jacqueline Jordan, 3

Johnson, Ray, 29, 41, 46, 47, 50, 52
Jordan, William Chester, 9
Journal of Blacks in Higher Education, 21

Karenga, Maulana, 15, 16, 23, 44
Kreisberg, Seth, 25, 27, 66, 71, 72
Kunjufu, Jawanza, 14, 55, 74

Leake, B. L., 32
Leake, D. O., 32
Lessons From Black History, 55
Luttwak, Edward N., 21

Madhubuti, Haki, 72, 73
Majors, Richard, 63, 76
Malcolm X African American Immersion, Milwaukee, 32, 62
Malcolm X African-Centered Academy, Detroit, 31
male academy, 7
Man to Man, Detroit, 34, 36
Manhattan Institute, 20, 22
Manhood Incorporated, Detroit, 34, 36
Martin Luther King, Jr. African American Immersion Academy, Milwaukee , 32, 62
Marxist critiques, 4
Matthew A. Henson Elementary School, Baltimore, 33
McGriff, Deborah, 14
McNeil, Linda, 4, 81
Morehouse Mentoring Program, Atlanta, 38, 39
"My Brother's Keeper" Program, East Lansing, xi, 34, 36

National Association for the Advancement of Colored People, 8, 25, 26

National Assessment of Educational Progress, 3

National Coalition of Advocates for Students, 2

National Education Association, 10

National Organization of Women's Education and Defense Fund, 12, 14, 19, 25, 26, 31, 49, 53, 112

National Urban League, 3

North Carolina Public Schools, x

Ogbu, John, 72

Paul Robeson African-Centered Academy, Detroit, 31

Phillips, Marian, 8, 74

Pine Villa Elementary School, Dade County, 33

PROJECT ALPHA, 38

Project 2000, Baltimore, 34, 37

Ravitch, Diane, 21

RAAMUS Academy, Cincinnati, 38, 39

Robert Coleman Elementary School, Baltimore, 33

Robert L. Fulton Middle School, 33

Sadker, David, 15, 16–20

Sadker, Myra, 15, 16–20

"Save A Star" Male Leadership Development, Detroit, 34, 37

Sheffield, Horace, Jr., 8

Simon, Howard, 13

Soderman, Anne K., 8, 74

Solomon, R. Patrick, 63, 64, 68

Sparks, Anita, 41

Smitherman, Geneva, xi, 11, 31, 41, 74

Stanton Elementary School, Washington, D.C., 33

State of Black America, 2, 3, 4

Title IX of the 1972 Education Amendment, 12

Toussaint Institute Fund, Inc., New York, 38

Truely, Walteen, 12

Ujamma Institute-Medgar Evers College, New York, 32

U.S. Census Bureau, 3

Vega, Marta Moreno, 24

Wake County Public Schools, 34, 35

Watson, Clifford, xi, 11, 29, 31, 41, 42, 43, 45, 74

Weis, Lois, 71, 72

West, Cornel, 21

Whitaker, 52

Wiley, Ed, III, 15

Willis, 72

Woods, George, ix

Woodson, Carter G., 7

Wynn, Mychal, 104

Yates, Alfred, 8